FATAL FURY: CITY OF THE WOLVES GAME GUIDE

Table of Contents

CHAPTER 1: INTRODUCTION TO FATAL FURY: CITY OF THE WOLVES

1.1   Overview of the Fatal Fury Series

The *Fatal Fury* series is one of the most iconic fighting game franchises developed by SNK. Debuting in 1991 with the release of *Fatal Fury: King of Fighters*, it quickly became a hallmark of arcade fighting games during the 90s and helped solidify SNK's place in the competitive gaming market.

1. The Birth of Fatal Fury (1991)
The first *Fatal Fury* introduced players to the world of South Town, a fictional city known for its underground fighting tournaments. The game featured a cast of characters who would become staples of SNK's fighting games, including Terry Bogard, Andy Bogard, Joe Higashi, and the villainous Geese Howard. It also introduced a groundbreaking two-plane battle system, where players could move between the foreground and background, creating dynamic combat strategies and a sense of depth not seen in many other fighters at the time.

2. Success and Legacy
Fatal Fury became one of the most popular fighting franchises of the early 90s, with multiple sequels and spin-offs, including *Fatal Fury 2* (1992), *Fatal Fury Special* (1993), *Fatal Fury 3: Road to the Final Victory* (1995), and *Fatal Fury: Wild Ambition* (1999). Each entry improved on the gameplay mechanics, adding new characters, stages, and techniques, while maintaining the series' trademark innovation in battle mechanics.

In 1993, SNK also launched the *King of Fighters* series, which initially featured characters from *Fatal Fury* alongside other SNK franchises, and eventually became a standalone game series. Despite *King of Fighters* growing in prominence, *Fatal Fury* continued to maintain a loyal fanbase.

3. Key Features of the Franchise

- **Iconic Characters:** Terry Bogard remains one of the most iconic characters in the history of fighting games. Over time, characters like Mai Shiranui, Rock Howard, and Geese Howard became symbols of the SNK brand.
- **Battle System Innovation:** The two-plane system introduced in the first game was a significant innovation in the fighting game genre. The series also pioneered various system mechanics like counterattacks, special moves, and a focus on unique character abilities.
- **Storytelling:** The narrative of *Fatal Fury* revolves around the struggles of Terry Bogard and his quest for revenge against Geese Howard, who killed his father. Throughout the series, characters grow, form alliances, and confront personal vendettas, with South Town and its inhabitants forming the backdrop to many of the game's events.

4. Fatal Fury in the Modern Era

While the *Fatal Fury* franchise initially found its place in the 90s arcades, it has transitioned well into modern gaming. Characters from *Fatal Fury* have appeared in several *King of Fighters* installments and spin-off games. The series continues to influence fighting game design today, and its legacy is honored in modern SNK titles such as *King of Fighters XIV* and *Samurai Shodown* (2019).

The *Fatal Fury* series' impact can be seen not just in gameplay but in the larger fighting game community. Its characters, mechanics, and its representation of SNK's unique approach to arcade gaming remain a testament to its lasting influence on the genre. The upcoming *Fatal Fury: City of the Wolves* marks a new chapter in this storied franchise, offering a fresh look while honoring the legacy of the original games.

1.2   Setting and Storyline

The *Fatal Fury* series is set in a world filled with underground fighting tournaments, criminal organizations, and intense rivalries. The central backdrop for many of the games is South Town, a fictional city that serves as the heart of much of the series' events. Over the years, the narrative evolves through multiple sequels and spin-offs, weaving a complex and engaging story filled with personal vendettas, familial ties, and larger-than-life battles.

South Town: The Heart of the Conflict

South Town is a dangerous, crime-ridden metropolis where the most brutal fighting tournaments take place. The city's underworld is controlled by powerful figures, and it's often the battleground for fierce rivalries between legendary fighters. South Town serves as the starting point for many of the storylines, where characters like Terry Bogard, Andy Bogard, and Mai Shiranui battle their way through its criminal syndicates and fight for justice.

The Story of Terry Bogard and Geese Howard

The primary storyline of the *Fatal Fury* series centers around Terry Bogard, the series' main protagonist, and his quest for vengeance against Geese Howard, the man responsible for the death of his father, Jeff Bogard. This personal vendetta is the driving force behind the events of the original *Fatal Fury* game.

In the first game, Terry and his brother Andy participate in the King of Fighters tournament to avenge their father's death, which was orchestrated by the ruthless Geese Howard. As they progress through the tournament, they encounter numerous fighters who each have their own motivations and reasons for participating in the battle.

The Rise of Geese Howard

Geese Howard, the primary antagonist of the *Fatal Fury* series, is a ruthless and power-hungry crime lord who controls South Town with an iron fist. His ability to manipulate people, including his own family, makes him a formidable foe. Geese's influence stretches across the city's underworld, and he continues to be a central figure in the conflict. His appearance in various *King of Fighters* titles and *Fatal Fury* sequels cements him as one of the most iconic villains in fighting game history.

The Bogard Brothers' Journey

While the original game focuses heavily on Terry's personal vendetta against Geese, the storyline of *Fatal Fury* expands to include his brother Andy and his companions, like Joe Higashi and Mai Shiranui. Andy, with his own set of motivations and fighting style, often serves as a foil to Terry, especially with his calm demeanor compared to Terry's more brash and determined nature. Their bond, as well as the relationships they form with other fighters, is a key part of the series' emotional depth.

As the games progress, characters like Rock Howard, Geese's son, come into the story, adding complexity and new layers to the narrative. Rock struggles with his own identity, torn between his inherited fighting skills and his desire to avoid his father's ruthless legacy. His role in *Fatal Fury: Mark of the Wolves* introduced an exciting new chapter in the *Fatal Fury* saga, as Rock becomes a symbol of hope for the future.

Major Story Arcs

- **The King of Fighters Tournament:** This is the central event in the early games, where fighters from around the world come together to compete for the title and settle their personal scores. Each tournament brings new characters and conflicts to the forefront, as well as unique plotlines that tie into the overarching narrative of South Town's crime syndicate.
- **Geese's Empire:** Throughout the series, Geese Howard's quest for absolute power serves as a major storyline. His machinations impact not only South Town but the larger world of *Fatal Fury*. He frequently seeks to expand his influence, manipulating fighters and political figures to achieve his goals. In *Fatal Fury 3*, Geese's attempts to control the world's most powerful fighters takes a backseat to new villains and threats, though his shadow looms large over the events.
- **The Howard Legacy:** Rock Howard's emergence as the son of Geese introduces a complex family dynamic to the

story. He is initially presented as a reluctant heir to his father's dark legacy, but as the story unfolds, Rock becomes a pivotal character in the series, representing a new generation of fighters seeking to forge their own path away from their parents' sins.

The Enduring Conflict

Despite numerous sequels and spin-offs, the core of the *Fatal Fury* series remains Terry's struggle against Geese and the larger fight against the corruption of South Town. New characters, storylines, and settings have expanded the narrative, but the conflict between good and evil, and the personal journeys of the characters, have remained consistent themes.

As the franchise continues with titles like *Fatal Fury: City of the Wolves*, these themes evolve, and characters from past games are revisited, further deepening the complex relationships that have defined the *Fatal Fury* universe.

4o mini

1.3   Key Features of City of the Wolves

Fatal Fury: City of the Wolves marks the return of the beloved *Fatal Fury* series with a host of exciting new features, while staying true to the core elements that fans of the franchise have come to love. This new installment brings innovative gameplay mechanics, a fresh narrative, and enhanced visuals to both longtime fans and newcomers. Here's a look at the key features that define *City of the Wolves*:

1. A New Generation of Fighters

One of the most exciting aspects of *City of the Wolves* is the introduction of a new cast of characters alongside some returning fan favorites. The story revolves around Rock Howard, the son of Geese Howard, as he grapples with his legacy and personal growth. Players can expect new heroes and villains with unique fighting styles, backgrounds, and abilities. These new fighters bring fresh dynamics to the gameplay, offering players a broader array of strategies to explore.

- **Rock Howard**: As the central character, Rock offers a perfect blend of power and technique, mixing his inherited skills from both his father and his adoptive father, Terry Bogard.
- **New Challengers**: *City of the Wolves* introduces fresh faces, each with their own motives for entering the King of Fighters tournament. Some of these characters bring exotic fighting styles and abilities that shake up the usual tactics seen in past games.

2. Revamped Battle Mechanics

The core of any *Fatal Fury* game lies in its battle mechanics, and *City of the Wolves* takes this to the next level with the introduction of the **REV System** (Revolutionary Enhanced Victory System). This system is designed to offer more strategic depth in battles, giving players the ability to change their approach depending on the situation. Some of the key battle features include:

- **Dual Fighting Planes**: Building on the series' original concept, players can still switch between the foreground and background, creating opportunities for strategic positioning and evasion during combat.
- **REV System**: The REV System rewards skilled players who can chain together high-level combos and perform counterattacks at the right moments. This new mechanic allows for more dramatic, high-impact finishes, providing players with a deeper and more rewarding combat experience.
- **Hyper Combos & Special Techniques**: The game features visually stunning, high-damage combos, and special moves, which not only deal significant damage but can also shift the momentum of a fight.

3. Enhanced Visuals and Art Style

Fatal Fury: City of the Wolves benefits from a significant upgrade in terms of graphics and visual presentation. The game utilizes modern technology to bring its characters, stages, and animations to life in breathtaking detail. Key visual upgrades include:

- **Stylized 2D Character Sprites with 3D Backgrounds**: The game retains the traditional 2D sprite style that fans of *Fatal Fury* love but now features 3D backgrounds, adding layers of depth and immersion to each arena. The combination of 2D characters and 3D environments offers a dynamic and cinematic feel to the action.
- **Fluid Animation and Effects**: The animation quality has been enhanced, allowing for smoother transitions between moves, and adding explosive visual effects for special attacks, giving fights a more epic and cinematic feel.

- **Environmental Interactions**: Certain stages in *City of the Wolves* are designed with interactive elements, allowing characters to engage with their surroundings, adding new layers of strategy and unpredictability to each battle.

4. Expanded Story Mode and Multiple Endings

The story mode in *Fatal Fury: City of the Wolves* offers players an immersive experience as they follow Rock Howard's journey to confront his past and his identity. Unlike earlier entries, the game introduces branching narratives with multiple endings, allowing players to make choices that will affect the course of the story and how it concludes. Features of the expanded story mode include:

- **Character-driven Storylines**: Each fighter has their own personal storyline that players can explore. These story arcs delve deeper into the motivations of the characters, including Rock's struggle with his father's legacy and his own path to self-discovery.
- **Multiple Endings**: Depending on player choices and actions during key moments in the story, players can unlock different endings, offering replayability and varied experiences.
- **Cinematic Cutscenes**: Throughout the story mode, players will enjoy beautifully animated cutscenes that push the narrative forward. These scenes provide additional context for the characters and the overarching plot, immersing players in the world of South Town and beyond.

5. Online Multiplayer and Community Features

Taking advantage of modern technology, *City of the Wolves* offers a robust online multiplayer experience that allows players to face off against others around the world. The game introduces several new features to enhance its online capabilities:

- **Ranked and Casual Matches**: Players can engage in both ranked competitive matches and casual encounters, allowing for a variety of playstyles and skill levels to be accommodated.
- **Tournaments and Events**: Online tournaments and special events offer players a chance to compete for exclusive rewards, trophies, and bragging rights.
- **Fighter Profiles and Leaderboards**: Players can track their stats and see where they rank against the global community. Leaderboards provide a sense of accomplishment and competition, with regular updates showcasing the top players in various categories.

6. DLC and Post-Launch Content

Fatal Fury: City of the Wolves is designed to evolve after its initial release, with a variety of downloadable content (DLC) planned. This includes additional characters, stages, costumes, and new gameplay modes that will keep the community engaged long after launch. Features of the post-launch content include:

- **DLC Fighters**: New characters will be introduced in the form of DLC packs, expanding the roster with exciting new fighters and returning favorites.

- **Season Pass**: Players can purchase a season pass that grants access to all major updates and expansions, ensuring they won't miss out on any new content.
- **Customization Options**: Customization features, such as new skins, taunts, and victory poses, will allow players to personalize their fighters in unique ways.

1.4   New Additions and Innovations

Fatal Fury: City of the Wolves introduces several exciting additions and innovative features that set it apart from previous entries in the series, while staying true to the franchise's core identity. These new elements offer fresh gameplay mechanics, expanded storylines, and advanced technology to enhance the overall player experience. Here's a look at some of the most notable additions and innovations:

1. The REV System (Revolutionary Enhanced Victory System)

One of the standout innovations in *City of the Wolves* is the **REV System**, a new combat mechanic designed to provide deeper, more dynamic battles. The REV System adds a new layer of strategy to each fight, rewarding skilled players who can manage their meter and execute moves at the right moments. Key elements of the REV System include:

- **Victory Points**: Players build a "REV meter" by executing successful attacks, combos, and counters. This meter can be activated for a powerful "REV Burst," a temporary boost that enhances the player's speed, attack power, and special move effectiveness.

- **REV Combos**: Players can link moves into special REV Combos that trigger devastating attacks. These combos are visually striking and highly rewarding, making timing and precision critical for success.
- **Strategic Depth**: The system encourages players to carefully manage their REV meter throughout the fight, deciding when to activate it for maximum advantage. Whether to use it early for an edge or save it for a crucial moment adds an exciting strategic element to every match.

2. Expanded Roster of Fighters

In *City of the Wolves*, the character roster has been significantly expanded, introducing both new fighters and beloved returning characters with updated moves and abilities. These additions offer players more diverse gameplay options and strategies. Some of the key roster innovations include:

- **Rock Howard**: The game's central character, Rock Howard, carries forward his father's legacy but with a more refined fighting style. Rock's moves blend elements of Terry and Geese's techniques, allowing players to perform unique combos and special moves.
- **New Fighters**: A new wave of characters brings exciting fresh faces to the *Fatal Fury* universe, each with their own fighting style, personality, and backstory. These new fighters add variety to the roster, ranging from martial artists to street brawlers with distinct movesets.
- **Legacy Characters with New Moves**: Classic characters such as Terry Bogard, Mai Shiranui, and Andy Bogard return with updated move sets and improved animations,

making them feel both nostalgic and fresh for long-time fans of the series.

3. Interactive Environments and Stage Hazards

One of the most innovative additions to *City of the Wolves* is the inclusion of **interactive environments** and **stage hazards**. In previous *Fatal Fury* games, stages were largely static backgrounds for battles. However, *City of the Wolves* takes it a step further with dynamic, interactive elements that impact the flow of combat. These features include:

- **Environmental Interactions**: Some stages feature objects that players can interact with during a fight. This could mean bouncing off walls for a surprise attack or breaking objects to cause temporary changes in the battlefield, like altering the layout of the environment or momentarily stunning opponents.
- **Stage Hazards**: Certain arenas include environmental hazards that affect the match, such as falling debris, fire traps, or changes in weather that alter how certain moves behave. Players must adapt to these dynamic conditions, making each battle feel more unpredictable and exciting.
- **Destructible Stages**: In some stages, the environment can be damaged during the course of a fight, leading to dramatic changes as the match progresses. These destructible elements add a new layer of immersion and provide players with new strategies to exploit.

4. Character Customization and Gear

In response to the growing demand for personalized experiences, *City of the Wolves* introduces extensive **character customization** options that allow players to modify their fighters both aesthetically and functionally. This system is designed to give players more control over how they engage in battles. Some customization features include:

- **Costume Variations**: Players can unlock and equip different outfits, accessories, and visual effects for each character. Whether it's new gear or alternate costumes, players can create their own unique look for their favorite fighters.
- **Move Customization**: In addition to aesthetic changes, players can modify certain aspects of their character's move set, adjusting the timing, speed, and properties of moves. This allows for a more tailored fighting style suited to individual preferences.
- **Victory Poses and Taunts**: Custom victory poses and taunts allow players to personalize their fighters' celebratory animations after winning a round. These can be unlocked and equipped, giving players a chance to showcase their personal style during matches.

5. Advanced AI and Challenge Modes

The AI in *City of the Wolves* has been significantly improved to offer more challenging and varied fights. This makes single-player modes more engaging, especially for players who want to practice or enjoy the game without necessarily going online. Some of the key AI innovations include:

- **Smart AI Behavior**: Enemies now adapt to player strategies, learning from their actions and adjusting accordingly. This means that players can no longer rely on the same strategies repeatedly; the AI forces players to evolve their tactics and fight smarter.

- **Challenge Modes**: New challenge modes have been added to test players' skills in creative ways. These modes present unique scenarios where players must fight under certain constraints, like limited health, time, or special conditions. They offer additional rewards and unlockables upon completion.
- **Tactical Difficulty Scaling**: As players progress, the game's difficulty dynamically adjusts to provide an appropriate challenge. The system ensures that fights are neither too easy nor frustratingly difficult, allowing players of all skill levels to find success without feeling overwhelmed.

6. Enhanced Online Features

With *City of the Wolves*, SNK is expanding its online capabilities to foster a thriving global community. These features aim to improve multiplayer experiences, increase player engagement, and provide more competitive avenues for fans of the series. Key innovations include:

- **Online Ranking and Leaderboards**: Players can now compete against one another on a global scale through a detailed ranking system. Leaderboards are divided by region and skill level, giving players a sense of accomplishment as they rise through the ranks.
- **Tournaments and Events**: Regular online tournaments and special in-game events keep the community active and engaged, offering players the chance to compete for exclusive rewards and seasonal content.
- **Spectator Mode**: This mode allows players to watch live matches of others, including top-ranked players, and

learn from their techniques. It's an excellent way to improve by observing high-level play.

CHAPTER 2: GETTING STARTED

2.1 Installation and Setup

Getting *Fatal Fury: City of the Wolves* up and running is an essential first step for players looking to dive into the action. Whether you're playing on PC, console, or an arcade machine, the installation and setup process is straightforward but varies slightly depending on the platform. Below is a step-by-step guide to ensure a smooth installation and setup experience.

1. Installation on PC (Steam, Epic Games, or other platforms)

- **Step 1: Purchase and Download**
    - Go to your preferred digital storefront (Steam, Epic Games Store, etc.).
    - Search for *Fatal Fury: City of the Wolves* and purchase the game.
    - Once purchased, click on the download button to start the download process.
- **Step 2: Install the Game**
    - After the download is complete, the installation should begin automatically.
    - If prompted, choose the installation directory. It's recommended to install the game on your primary drive unless you have limited space.
    - Follow any on-screen prompts to complete the installation process.
- **Step 3: Launching the Game**
    - After installation is complete, launch the game either through the platform's client (Steam, Epic Games) or directly from your desktop if a shortcut was created.

- The first time you run the game, it may prompt you to set up basic preferences like display resolution and controls. Make sure to adjust these settings according to your system and comfort.

2. Installation on Consoles (PlayStation, Xbox, Nintendo Switch)

- **Step 1: Purchase and Download/Insert Disc**
  - If you purchased a physical disc, insert it into your console.
  - If you bought a digital version, navigate to the PlayStation Store, Xbox Store, or Nintendo eShop, search for *Fatal Fury: City of the Wolves*, and purchase it.
  - Download the game to your console's hard drive (or an external drive, depending on available space).
- **Step 2: Install the Game**
  - For physical copies, the installation will start automatically once the disc is inserted.
  - For digital copies, the game will begin downloading as soon as the purchase is complete. Ensure you have enough free space on your console.
- **Step 3: Launching the Game**
  - Once the installation is finished, the game will be available in your console's library or home screen.
  - Select the game to launch, and you'll be taken to the main menu where you can begin your adventure.

3. Arcade Machine Setup (For Arcade Versions)

If you're playing the arcade version of *Fatal Fury: City of the Wolves*, setting up the machine involves configuring the hardware and ensuring the software is properly installed.

- **Step 1: Powering Up the Machine**
  - Plug in the arcade machine and power it on.
  - If it's a brand-new unit, follow the included manual for initial setup.
- **Step 2: Software Installation**
  - Arcade units typically come with the game pre-installed. If not, the software can be loaded via USB or disc drive based on the machine's specifications.
  - Follow on-screen instructions to install the game. Ensure all files are transferred and installed properly.
- **Step 3: Calibrating the Controls**
  - Configure the controls (joysticks and buttons) to match the expected input for the game.
  - Test the setup to ensure the buttons and movements are responsive.

4. Updating the Game

- After installation, it's important to check for any available updates or patches that improve gameplay, fix bugs, or add new features.
  - On PC, Steam and Epic Games usually update the game automatically, but it's always good to check the game's settings menu for manual updates.
  - On consoles, go to the game's options in your system's menu and select "Check for Updates."

o   For arcade units, updates may require a USB stick or network connection to download the latest patch.

5. System Requirements (For PC Players)

If you're playing on PC, ensure that your system meets the minimum or recommended requirements for a smooth experience:

- **Operating System**: Windows 10 or later / macOS (latest versions)
- **Processor**: Intel Core i5-9600K or AMD Ryzen 5 3600
- **Memory**: 8 GB RAM
- **Graphics**: Nvidia GTX 1060 / AMD Radeon RX 570 or better
- **Storage**: 20 GB available space
- **Sound**: DirectX compatible sound card

Ensure your system meets or exceeds these requirements for optimal performance.

2.2 Navigating the Main Menu

Once the game is installed and launched, you'll be greeted by the main menu, which serves as the central hub from which all aspects of *Fatal Fury: City of the Wolves* can be accessed. The menu is designed to be intuitive and streamlined, allowing players to quickly jump into the action or explore additional features.

1. Main Menu Layout

- **Start Game**: This option lets you jump directly into the main gameplay modes such as Story Mode, Arcade Mode, or Online Play. Selecting this will bring up a secondary menu to choose which mode you'd like to play.
- **Options**: This section allows you to adjust various settings related to gameplay, audio, graphics, and controls. Common options include:
    - **Graphics Settings**: Adjust screen resolution, display mode (windowed/full-screen), and other visual enhancements (e.g., anti-aliasing, V-Sync).
    - **Audio Settings**: Adjust the volume for music, sound effects, and voice acting. You can also toggle subtitles for in-game dialogue.
    - **Controls**: Customize your control scheme for both keyboard (PC) and gamepad (console). You can remap buttons to your liking or select from predefined presets.
- **Game Modes**: This section houses the various game modes available, such as:
    - **Story Mode**: Embark on the narrative-driven journey of *City of the Wolves* and experience Rock Howard's rise.
    - **Arcade Mode**: Compete against AI opponents in a series of matches, eventually facing off against the final boss.
    - **Survival Mode**: Fight against waves of enemies to see how long you can last.
    - **Training Mode**: Practice your combos, moves, and strategies against a dummy opponent in a no-pressure environment.
- **Online**: This option connects you to online features, where you can engage in multiplayer battles, participate

in ranked matches, or take part in tournaments and community events. Key sections here include:

- ○ **Ranked Matches**: Face off against players around the world and climb the leaderboards.
- ○ **Casual Matches**: Play unranked, fun matches with friends or random players.
- ○ **Tournaments**: Join organized online tournaments and compete for prizes and bragging rights.
- **Gallery**: Unlock and view in-game content such as character artwork, cinematic cutscenes, concept art, and more. These are typically unlocked by completing specific challenges or progressing through the game's story.
- **Extras**: This section may contain additional content such as downloadable content (DLC), seasonal updates, or challenges that you can download or purchase to expand your experience.
- **Exit**: This option lets you exit the game and return to your system's home screen or shutdown menu.

2. Submenus and Navigation Tips

When navigating the main menu, it's important to familiarize yourself with the submenu structure:

- **Arrow Navigation**: Use the directional pad or arrows to navigate through the options. On PC, you can use your mouse, but for smoother navigation, the keyboard or controller may be more efficient.
- **Confirming Selections**: Once an option is highlighted, press the corresponding action button (e.g., X on PlayStation, A on Xbox, Enter on PC) to confirm your selection. For canceling or going back, press the designated "Back" button (e.g., Circle on PlayStation, B on Xbox).

- **Tooltips**: For more details on certain options, such as control settings or gameplay modes, hover over them to display tooltips or information on what they entail.

3. Quick Access Features

In the main menu, you'll find quick access buttons at the bottom of the screen or in the corner, depending on your platform. These might include:

- **Notifications**: Alerts for new updates, DLCs, or upcoming events.
- **Social Features**: Links to the game's official community, where you can interact with other players, watch streams, or check out community tournaments.

Navigating the main menu is simple, and once you get familiar with the layout, you'll be able to jump straight into the action with ease. Enjoy your journey through *Fatal Fury: City of the Wolves*!

2.3 Understanding Game Modes

Fatal Fury: City of the Wolves offers a variety of game modes that cater to different playstyles, from story-driven experiences to competitive multiplayer battles. Understanding the purpose and structure of each game mode will help you choose the right one based on your preferences, whether you're seeking a deep narrative, casual play, or challenging competitive action. Below is an overview of the key game modes available:

1. Story Mode

Story Mode is the centerpiece of *City of the Wolves*, immersing players in the narrative-driven journey of Rock Howard as he struggles with his past and the legacy of his father, Geese Howard. In this mode, players can experience the plot from Rock's perspective, interact with other characters, and unlock special story events and endings based on choices made during the game.

- **Objectives**: Players advance through different chapters, facing various characters and bosses as they uncover more about Rock's story.
- **Branching Paths**: The decisions you make during key moments may influence how the story unfolds, leading to multiple possible endings.
- **Character Interactions**: Throughout Story Mode, you'll interact with familiar faces such as Terry Bogard, Mai Shiranui, and other characters, whose relationships with Rock evolve as the plot progresses.

2. Arcade Mode

Arcade Mode is a traditional fighting experience where you face off against a series of increasingly difficult AI-controlled opponents. It's perfect for players who want to test their skills against a variety of fighters without the narrative focus of Story Mode.

- **Structure**: You'll battle through a set number of opponents, culminating in a showdown with a final boss.

- **Difficulty Levels**: Arcade Mode allows players to select from various difficulty levels, ranging from easy to hard, depending on your experience and skill level.
- **Score Tracking**: Your performance is often tracked in terms of speed and accuracy, providing an extra layer of competition. The faster you defeat opponents or the fewer hits you take, the higher your score.

3. Survival Mode

In Survival Mode, players face wave after wave of enemies, testing how long they can last against increasingly difficult opponents. This mode is ideal for players looking for a test of endurance, as well as those seeking to hone their skills without the need for story progression.

- **Endless Waves**: Enemies come in waves, and each wave gets progressively harder. The objective is to survive for as long as possible.
- **Difficulty Scaling**: As you progress, enemies become stronger, requiring you to adapt your strategies to survive.
- **Rewards**: Survival Mode often rewards players based on the number of waves they complete, with special unlockables and achievements tied to high scores or endurance milestones.

4. Training Mode

Training Mode is designed to help players practice and perfect their moves without the pressure of an actual fight. Whether you're new to the game or a seasoned veteran, this mode offers an ideal environment to learn new combos, practice special techniques, and improve your timing.

- **Freeform Training**: In this mode, you can choose any character and engage in unlimited practice, focusing on any aspect of your gameplay.
- **Move Lists**: The game provides an accessible move list, showing you all the attacks, combos, and special moves that can be performed.
- **AI Assistance**: You can train with a dummy AI opponent that doesn't fight back, allowing you to practice without distractions. Some versions also let you record your moves and analyze your performance.

5. Versus Mode (Local Multiplayer)

Versus Mode allows you to engage in head-to-head battles with friends or family locally, either on the same console or through split-screen play. This mode is perfect for casual play or practice with others in a fun, non-competitive setting.

- **One-on-One Fights**: You and a friend can pick your characters and face off in direct combat. The winner stays, while the loser is replaced by the next player.
- **Character Selection**: Players can choose from the full roster of characters, including unlocked ones, depending on how far they are in the game.
- **No Story Progression**: Unlike Story Mode, Versus Mode doesn't follow a plot, so it's all about enjoying straightforward combat.

6. Online Multiplayer (Ranked and Casual Matches)

For players looking to compete with others worldwide, the Online Multiplayer modes are the way to go. These modes provide both competitive (Ranked) and casual (Quick Play) multiplayer matches, offering a chance to climb the leaderboards or simply have fun with other players.

- **Ranked Matches**: Compete against other players in ranked battles, where your performance determines your rank. Winning matches boosts your position, while losing may cause your rank to drop.
- **Casual Matches**: Play for fun in casual matches that don't affect your ranking. These are great for relaxing and practicing against real opponents.
- **Tournaments and Events**: Participate in online tournaments and seasonal events where players can earn special rewards and achievements.

7. Custom Game Modes (if available)

Fatal Fury: City of the Wolves may also feature customizable modes or special event modes, offering a variety of alternate playstyles such as:

- **Team Battles**: Fight in teams instead of one-on-one.
- **Survival Mode with a Twist**: Customize the survival mode with modifiers like time limits or handicaps for additional challenges.

Each mode provides a unique experience, catering to various types of players, from those seeking a deep story-driven experience to those looking for high-intensity competition.

2.4 Customizing Game Settings

Personalizing your *Fatal Fury: City of the Wolves* experience ensures that the game runs optimally on your system and fits your preferences. The game offers a range of settings for graphics, audio, controls, and gameplay, all of which can be adjusted in the "Options" menu.

1. Graphics Settings

For players on PC and consoles with graphical customization, adjusting the game's visuals can ensure the best possible performance or aesthetics based on your hardware.

- **Resolution**: Set the display resolution for optimal image quality. Higher resolutions provide sharper details but require more processing power.
- **Display Mode**: Choose between full-screen, windowed, or borderless window modes, depending on your preference for screen space or multi-tasking.
- **Graphics Quality**: Adjust the graphical settings such as texture quality, shadow quality, anti-aliasing, and more. Lowering some settings can help improve performance on lower-end systems.
- **V-Sync and Frame Rate Limit**: Enable V-Sync to reduce screen tearing and maintain a smooth frame rate, or adjust the frame rate limit if you're experiencing performance issues.

2. Audio Settings

The audio settings allow you to fine-tune your game's sound to suit your environment and preferences. Whether you want to hear every punch clearly or turn down background music, here's what you can adjust:

- **Music Volume**: Control the overall volume of in-game music.
- **Sound Effects Volume**: Adjust the volume of sound effects like punches, kicks, and special move sounds.
- **Voice Acting Volume**: If your version of the game includes voice acting, you can adjust the volume of in-game voices or mute them entirely.
- **Audio Output**: Choose between stereo and surround sound (if supported by your setup), or adjust it based on your speaker or headphone configuration.

3. Control Settings

Customize how the game responds to your input devices, whether you're using a controller, keyboard, or arcade stick. Key options in the control settings include:

- **Button Mapping**: Remap the default controls to suit your playstyle, especially if you're using a controller or gamepad. You can assign buttons to different functions, such as special attacks, block, or jump.
- **Joystick/Analog Sensitivity**: Adjust the sensitivity of your joystick or analog stick. This is important for players who prefer more control over their character's movement or want to fine-tune the responsiveness.

- **Invert Controls**: For those who prefer inverted controls (common in many flight or shooting games), you can switch the default axis for movement or camera controls.

4. Gameplay Settings

Adjust gameplay mechanics to suit your skill level or preferences:

- **Difficulty Level**: Choose the difficulty for AI opponents in modes like Story Mode or Arcade Mode. Options generally range from Easy, Normal, Hard, and Expert.
- **Assist Options**: Some games offer assist features for newer players, such as simplified combo inputs or automatic moves. Customize whether these assists are turned on or off to provide either a more accessible or challenging experience.
- **HUD Customization**: Customize the heads-up display (HUD) to adjust what information appears during gameplay, such as health bars, timer, or move lists.

5. Language and Region

If available, you can change the language and region settings of the game. This is useful if you prefer a different language for text or voice acting or need to set the game's region to match your local gaming servers for online play.

- **Language Settings**: Switch between multiple available languages for text, menus, and possibly voice acting.
- **Region Settings**: Some games have region-specific content or servers for online play. Adjusting this option may help you connect to a server closer to your geographic location for better ping and latency.

CHAPTER 3: GAME MODES EXPLAINED

3.1 Arcade Mode

Arcade Mode in *Fatal Fury: City of the Wolves* is a classic feature that lets players face off against a series of progressively difficult AI-controlled opponents. It offers an action-packed experience without the distraction of story elements, perfect for honing your skills or simply enjoying a quick bout.

- **Objective**: Progress through a series of stages, each featuring different characters with increasing difficulty. The ultimate goal is to reach the final boss and defeat them.
- **Structure**: Players select a character and battle through a set number of stages. Each victory earns you points and sometimes unlocks new challenges or hidden characters.
- **Difficulty Levels**: Choose from multiple difficulty settings such as Easy, Normal, and Hard. Higher difficulties present faster, more aggressive AI, challenging even experienced players.
- **Endings**: Completing Arcade Mode may unlock different endings depending on your performance and the characters you use, providing replay value.
- **Leaderboards**: Compete for the best times or highest scores and see how your performance stacks up against players around the world in global rankings.

3.2 Episodes of South Town

"Episodes of South Town" is a unique game mode that blends storytelling and fighting mechanics, allowing players to experience key moments from the *Fatal Fury* universe with a focus on South Town's notorious characters.

- **Storyline Integration**: This mode offers players a more narrative-driven experience, featuring a series of events and battles that follow the rich lore of South Town, where Geese Howard reigns as a powerful crime lord.
- **Character Focus**: Key characters like Terry Bogard, Mai Shiranui, and the iconic Geese Howard play central roles, with players battling against them to progress through the episodes. Each episode showcases the personal struggles and rivalries of these characters.
- **Branching Paths**: Some episodes include branching choices that can affect the outcome of the story, allowing you to explore different scenarios and alternate storylines.
- **Unlockables**: Completing certain episodes may unlock additional characters, special costumes, or lore-related content, enhancing the overall depth of the *Fatal Fury* universe.
- **Episodic Challenges**: Each episode often includes special challenges, such as defeating an opponent within a time limit or without using certain attacks, rewarding players with extra content.

3.3 Online Multiplayer

Online Multiplayer brings the competitive spirit of *Fatal Fury: City of the Wolves* to a global stage, allowing players to face off against others in real-time battles. This mode is ideal for those seeking an intense and engaging experience against human opponents.

- **Ranked Matches**: Engage in competitive battles where your performance affects your online rank. The better you perform, the higher you climb on the leaderboards. Ranked matches offer the thrill of competition, with players from all over the world.
- **Casual Matches**: For those looking to play without worrying about rankings, Casual Matches offer a more relaxed environment. You can still test your skills against real players, but the pressure of rankings is removed.
- **Online Tournaments**: Participate in special online events or tournaments that occur regularly. These competitions can lead to big rewards, such as exclusive skins, characters, or even prizes in some cases.
- **Matchmaking**: Online matchmaking ensures that you face opponents of similar skill levels, providing balanced and fair matches. The game automatically matches you with players within a close ranking range.
- **Co-op Modes**: Some online multiplayer modes allow for co-op play, where you and a friend can team up to tackle challenges or fight against other player teams.

3.4 Training and Practice Modes

The Training and Practice Modes are essential for players who want to improve their skills, master combos, and perfect their strategies before jumping into real fights. These modes allow for in-depth exploration of character abilities and move sets without the pressure of a competitive match.

- **Free Training**: This mode gives you complete freedom to practice any move or combo at your own pace. You can fight against an AI-controlled opponent who won't fight back, allowing you to focus on mastering your character's attacks.

- **Combo Practice**: Focus specifically on learning and perfecting your character's combos. The game may include a combo list, showing you the most effective combinations of moves, and you can replay them as many times as necessary to memorize the inputs.
- **AI Behavior**: In some versions of the training mode, you can adjust the AI's behavior. You can set the opponent to block, attack, or react in specific ways, providing a dynamic training environment.
- **Frame Data**: Advanced players can delve into frame data, which helps them understand the timing and recovery periods of different moves. This information is crucial for players who wish to optimize their techniques and maximize their effectiveness in battle.
- **Challenges**: Some training modes also include challenges or mini-games, such as performing a set number of perfect counters or executing a series of difficult combos in a time limit. Completing these challenges can reward you with achievements or unlockables.

Each of these modes provides a different aspect of gameplay, catering to various types of players, whether you're a seasoned veteran looking to practice advanced techniques or a newcomer learning the basics. Whether you prefer offline solo training or intense online competition, there's a mode to suit your needs.

CHAPTER 4: MASTERING THE BATTLE SYSTEM

4.1 Introduction to the REV System

The **REV System** is a key innovation in *Fatal Fury: City of the Wolves* that offers players an evolved approach to combat, bringing dynamic changes to how battles unfold. This system introduces new layers of strategy and depth, allowing for more tactical play and rewarding skilled execution.

- **What is the REV System?**
  The REV System (Revenge Energy Vortex) is a special mechanic designed to give players the opportunity to turn the tide of battle in critical moments. As players take damage, a REV meter builds up. When the meter is full, the player can activate a "REV" move, temporarily gaining enhanced abilities or access to powerful, game-changing techniques.
- **How REV Works:**
  - **REV Meter**: As you sustain damage or land attacks, your REV meter fills. The more damage you take, the faster the meter charges.
  - **Activation**: Once the REV meter is full, players can activate the REV mode, which triggers a temporary boost in strength, speed, and access to special moves.
  - **REV Power**: When activated, the REV mode provides access to super-powered versions of regular attacks, faster recovery times, or enhanced defensive capabilities. This makes it easier to punish opponents and regain control of the match, especially when you're at a disadvantage.

- **Strategic Use**:
  The REV System is not just about raw power; it's a tool for strategic play. A player who's trailing in health can use the REV to mount a comeback, using their temporary advantages to launch devastating attacks and turn the tide of battle. However, timing is crucial, as using REV at the wrong moment can leave you vulnerable when it runs out.
- **Countering REV**:
  Skilled opponents will learn to recognize when their opponent is close to activating REV and can plan accordingly to prevent its use or counter it with a well-timed attack. Understanding the REV System adds a deeper layer of strategy, especially in high-level play.

4.2 Classic Battle Mechanics

While the REV System brings a modern twist to combat, *Fatal Fury: City of the Wolves* also retains the **classic battle mechanics** that fans of the series know and love. These mechanics stay true to the roots of the *Fatal Fury* franchise, maintaining the core principles that have made it a beloved fighting game for years.

- **Two-Plane Fighting**:
  One of the key features of *Fatal Fury* and a staple of its battle mechanics is the **two-plane system**, which divides the screen into two fighting planes: foreground and background. Players can move between these planes to dodge attacks, reposition themselves, or create opportunities for combo setups. This system adds a layer of depth to movement, requiring players to think about both horizontal and vertical space during a fight.

- **Super Moves and Specials**:
  - **Super Moves**: Every character has access to powerful super moves that can deal massive damage when performed correctly. These moves typically require a combination of inputs and may consume a portion of the player's energy bar.
  - **Special Moves**: Each character in *City of the Wolves* has a unique set of special moves, which are usually faster, more damaging, and harder to block than regular attacks. Mastering the timing and distance of these moves is essential for successful gameplay.
- **Throw Mechanics**:
  Players can use throws to break an opponent's guard or close the gap when they're blocking too much. Throws are often performed when the opponent is too close, and they bypass traditional blocking, making them a powerful tool for offensive play. However, throws can be reversed or countered if the timing isn't right, so precision is key.
- **Blocking and Guarding**:
  A fundamental part of battle mechanics is the ability to **block** and **counter-block**. While blocking reduces damage, it also requires precise timing. Players can guard against incoming attacks, but if they hold the block button too long, they can be punished by throws or special attacks. **Counter-blocking**—timing your block to the moment your opponent attacks—can create openings for a quick counterattack.
- **Juggling and Combos**:
  Players who master the art of juggling can keep their opponent off the ground, stringing together a series of devastating attacks. The game's combo system rewards players who can time their attacks perfectly and chain multiple moves together without interruption.

- o **Air Juggling**: Some characters can juggle opponents mid-air, adding a layer of strategy to aerial combat.
- o **Ground Combos**: By using well-timed attacks, players can keep opponents on the ground and continue stringing together combos to maximize damage.
- **Speed and Timing**:
Classic battle mechanics emphasize the importance of speed and timing in *Fatal Fury: City of the Wolves*. Unlike games that focus solely on power, mastering the speed of attacks, blocks, and counters is essential. Characters with faster attack speeds can break through defenses or land combos before the opponent has a chance to react.
- **Character Diversity**:
The game's characters each have unique movesets and fighting styles, from powerful brawlers to agile martial artists. Each character's battle mechanics are designed to reflect their backstory and personality, which means players must learn each character's strengths and weaknesses to succeed.

4.3 Control Schemes: Arcade vs. Smart Style

In *Fatal Fury: City of the Wolves*, the control system is designed to cater to both seasoned veterans and new players, offering two distinct schemes: **Arcade** and **Smart Style**. Each system has its strengths, and choosing the right one can greatly influence your gameplay experience.

Arcade Control Scheme

The **Arcade** control scheme is designed for players who prefer a more traditional, skill-based experience, akin to the classic arcade fighting games. It emphasizes precision and depth, giving players full control over every aspect of their character's moves and actions.

- **Button Layout**:
    - Typically mapped to the standard **three-punch and three-kick buttons** (light, medium, and heavy) with an additional button for jumping and blocking.
    - Players must manually input complex combo commands and special move sequences, which rewards players with advanced knowledge of the game's mechanics.
- **Advanced Techniques**:
    - The **Arcade scheme** encourages mastery of advanced techniques such as **cancels, counter-attacks**, and **timing-based special moves**. To pull off combos and devastating moves, players need to input the correct sequence of moves within a limited window.
- **Depth and Customization**:
    - It offers full control over character movement, positioning, and advanced special techniques. Players have to memorize combos and execute them flawlessly, which appeals to competitive players who seek the challenge of mastering every aspect of gameplay.
- **Recommended For**:

o   Experienced players or those familiar with fighting games who want full control over their characters and enjoy a more challenging, technical playstyle.

Smart Style Control Scheme

The **Smart Style** control scheme, on the other hand, simplifies many of the inputs and makes special moves and combos more accessible for players who are newer to fighting games or prefer a less technical experience.

- **Button Layout**:
    - o   The **Smart Style** control scheme condenses the traditional button layout by mapping **special moves to single button presses**, often in combination with a direction on the joystick or d-pad.
    - o   This scheme reduces the need for precise timing and execution, as the game assists with input buffering, helping players land special moves and combos more easily.
- **Automatic Combos**:
    - o   The Smart Style system allows players to perform combos and special attacks with less effort, requiring fewer inputs to pull off the same moves. The game will "auto-combo" the sequence if you hit the correct pattern of directional inputs and buttons.
- **Assistive Features**:
    - o   Special moves may also be more forgiving in terms of input timing, with longer windows for executing them successfully.
- **Accessibility**:

- o This system is ideal for players who want to experience the full range of *Fatal Fury*'s moves but without the steep learning curve of manual execution. The Smart Style system makes fighting more accessible without sacrificing the excitement of the game.
- **Recommended For**:
    - o Beginners, casual players, or those who prefer a more straightforward and forgiving control system, allowing them to enjoy the game's combat mechanics without the pressure of mastering complex input sequences.

Which to Choose?

- **Arcade Style** is perfect for players who want to immerse themselves in the technical aspects of the game, offering deeper control and more satisfying mastery over combos and moves.
- **Smart Style** provides an easier entry point for those new to fighting games or who want to focus more on the action rather than technical precision.

4.4 Strategies for Combos and Special Moves

Mastering **combos and special moves** is central to becoming successful in *Fatal Fury: City of the Wolves*. Each character has a unique set of combos and devastating special moves that can deal huge damage and shift the momentum of a match. To get the most out of these techniques, here are some essential strategies for effectively using them.

1. Understanding Combo Chains

Combos are a sequence of attacks that, when performed correctly, allow you to continuously hit your opponent without giving them a chance to recover. Mastering combos is crucial for punishing your opponents and securing victory.

- **Light-to-Heavy Combos**:
  - A common strategy is to start with **light punches** or **kicks**, then transition into **medium or heavy attacks**. This is typically easier to perform, as it allows you to chain quick hits into stronger, more damaging attacks. The trick is maintaining fluidity and precision between each hit.
- **Combo Length and Timing**:
  - Short combos can be easier to execute, but longer combos do more damage. Timing is key here. Mastering the rhythm of your character's attacks will help you link multiple moves together without leaving a gap for the opponent to counter.
- **Launchers and Juggling**:
  - Some characters have **launching moves** that send opponents airborne, opening up the opportunity for **air juggle combos**. Practice juggling opponents in the air to extend combos and maximize damage.
- **Combo Practice**:
  - Use the game's **Training Mode** to practice and perfect your combos. Experiment with different combinations of light, medium, and heavy attacks to understand each character's range and timing.

2. Special Moves and Super Attacks

Special moves and super attacks are powerful tools that can give you the upper hand in any fight. These moves often have high damage potential, but they come with limitations like high energy costs or the need for precise inputs.

- **Know Your Character's Special Moves**:
  - Every character has a unique set of **special moves**, usually performed by inputting specific button combinations. Learning these moves is essential for maximizing your offensive strategy.
  - Special moves are often a mix of long-range attacks (like fireballs or projectiles) and close-range devastating strikes (like grabs or powerful punches).
- **Super Moves**:
  - Super Moves are the most powerful attacks in the game. They often require you to charge up energy or land specific hits in a sequence. Once you have enough energy or meet the right conditions, unleash your Super Move to deal massive damage.
  - Timing your Super Move correctly can be the difference between victory and defeat. Consider using them when your opponent's health is low or when you can easily punish their mistakes.
- **Energy Management**:
  - Special moves and Super Moves consume energy (REV meter or power gauge). Be mindful of when and how often you use them, as overusing them can leave you vulnerable in the long run.
  - **Counter Special Moves**: Some special moves can be **countered** by your opponent's special moves or

a well-timed block, so be strategic in when you deploy them.

3. Spacing and Timing for Special Moves

Even though special moves can be powerful, their effectiveness depends greatly on positioning and timing.

- **Range and Reach**:
    - Some special moves are long-range, while others are designed for close combat. Understanding the range of each of your character's special moves allows you to keep your distance or rush in at the right moment. For example, **fireball-type moves** are great for zoning and controlling the space between you and your opponent, while **dash attacks** are good for closing the gap.
- **Punishing Mistakes**:
    - If your opponent whiffs a move or is in the middle of an animation, it's the perfect time to unleash a special move. Pay attention to your opponent's patterns, and punish them when they leave themselves open.
- **Block and Counter**:
    - Some special moves can be blocked, but if you time your attacks correctly, you can **counter** or interrupt your opponent's special moves. This requires precise timing, but the reward is great — you can catch your opponent off guard and capitalize on their mistakes.

4. Character-Specific Strategies

Each character in *Fatal Fury: City of the Wolves* has a unique playstyle and set of strengths and weaknesses. Some characters are better suited for rushdown tactics, while others excel in zoning or counterplay.

- **Rushdown Tactics**:
    - Aggressive characters benefit from **rushdown strategies**, using fast, overwhelming attacks to pressure the opponent and force them into mistakes. These characters rely on quick combos, special moves, and constant pressure.
- **Zoning**:
    - Zoning characters, on the other hand, thrive on keeping their opponents at a distance with projectiles and long-range attacks. Focus on creating space and forcing your opponent to engage on your terms.
- **Defensive Play**:
    - Some characters excel at **counterplay**, relying on precise blocking, counters, and punishes to win fights. These characters require patience and an understanding of when to strike back.

By understanding how to implement these strategies for **combos and special moves**, you'll be able to maximize your potential in each fight, making you a formidable force in the arena of *Fatal Fury: City of the Wolves*.

CHAPTER 5: CHARACTER PROFILES

5.1 Rock Howard

Rock Howard, the son of the infamous Geese Howard, is one of the central characters in *Fatal Fury: City of the Wolves* and an iconic figure in the series. His fighting style combines powerful strikes with a mix of martial arts techniques, making him a versatile and dangerous opponent.

Backstory

- **Heritage**: As the son of Geese Howard, Rock initially carries the weight of his father's legacy, but he strives to create his own path, separate from the shadow of his father's criminal empire. His story revolves around his inner conflict and quest for identity, struggling to reconcile his bloodline with his desire to live a more honorable life.
- **Personality**: Rock's personality is a mixture of toughness and vulnerability. He is a serious fighter with a sense of justice, yet is often haunted by the darker aspects of his past. His growth as a character is reflected in his increasingly strong resolve to make his own destiny, free from his father's influence.

Fighting Style

- **Mix of Martial Arts and Street Fighting**:
  Rock's fighting style blends traditional martial arts with a more gritty, street-fighting approach. His moves focus on high-speed attacks, hard-hitting punches, and quick

counters, which make him a well-rounded character suited for both offensive and defensive strategies.

- **Rev Moves and Special Attacks**:
Rock's **Rev Moves** often revolve around enhanced versions of his classic strikes. His **Genocide Cutter** and **Raging Storm** are devastating super moves, capable of dealing massive damage if used correctly. When his REV meter is activated, Rock can turn the tide of battle with a powerful boost to his speed and damage output.
- **Unique Techniques**:
  - **Reversal Attacks**: Rock can perform quick reversal moves that allow him to counter his opponent's attacks with devastating force, making him effective against opponents who rely on high-pressure tactics.
  - **Projectiles**: Rock can also unleash projectiles, such as his **Reppuken**, to create distance or pressure his opponent from afar. This allows him to mix up his attacks and keep opponents guessing.
- **Playstyle**:
Rock excels in mid-range combat, using his quick movements and solid combo strings to overwhelm opponents. While he doesn't rely solely on zoning, his ability to quickly close the gap with special moves or throws makes him dangerous at any range.

Strengths and Weaknesses

- **Strengths**:
  - High damage output with super moves like **Raging Storm**.
  - Great mix of offense and defense, capable of keeping opponents on the backfoot.

- o Balanced move set that suits aggressive players who enjoy offensive strategies.
- **Weaknesses:**
  - o Not the fastest character in the game, so opponents who specialize in quick movements or zoning can challenge him.
  - o His special moves can be difficult to land against skilled players who anticipate them.

Strategic Tips for Rock

- **Mix Up Your Approach**: Rock's strength lies in his ability to adapt. Mix up quick strikes, projectiles, and special moves to create confusion and force your opponent into defensive positions.
- **Use REV Strategically**: Activate your REV meter when you're on the verge of losing momentum. Once activated, you'll be able to land devastating combo finishers and overpower your opponent.
- **Close the Distance Quickly**: Since Rock's best moves shine at close range, it's essential to close the distance quickly with special moves like **Raging Storm** or **Reppuken**, or by baiting your opponent into making a mistake you can punish.

5.2 Terry Bogard

Terry Bogard is perhaps one of the most iconic characters in the *Fatal Fury* series and a central figure in *City of the Wolves*. Known for his cheerful attitude, powerful fighting style, and signature moves, Terry is a fan-favorite who has become synonymous with the *Fatal Fury* franchise.

Backstory

- **The Hero of South Town**: Terry is a former street fighter who has dedicated his life to avenging the death of his adoptive father, Jeff Bogard, at the hands of Geese Howard. His determination to bring justice to South Town and protect his friends has earned him the respect and admiration of countless fighters and fans.
- **Personality**: Terry is known for his optimistic and energetic personality. Despite the hardships he's faced, he remains steadfast in his quest to bring peace to South Town. His signature phrase, "Are you okay?", is a testament to his sense of responsibility and care for others.

Fighting Style

- **Powerful Strikes and Quick Reactions**:
  Terry's fighting style is centered on strong, hard-hitting moves with high impact, focusing on solid strikes and explosive attacks. His moves are simple to perform but devastating when executed correctly.
- **Special Moves**:
  - **Power Wave**: Terry's **Power Wave** is one of his most iconic moves, a ground-based projectile that can be used to control space and force opponents to approach him. It's particularly effective at mid-range.
  - **Burn Knuckle**: His **Burn Knuckle** is a fast, close-range attack that allows him to rush toward his opponent with a powerful punch. It's a great tool for closing distance quickly.
  - **Crack Shoot**: A quick spinning kick that can be used to counter opponents who are too close,

Crack Shoot is ideal for punishing a blocked move or dodging an incoming attack.

- o **Power Dunk**: Terry's **Power Dunk** is a super move where he leaps into the air and slams his opponent with a powerful dive attack. It's an excellent way to punish opponents who rely on jumping attacks.
- o **Rising Tackle**: Terry's **Rising Tackle** is a vertical anti-air move that can knock out opponents trying to jump over him.
- **Super Moves**:
  - o **Buster Wolf**: Terry's **Buster Wolf** is his most devastating super move. It's a close-range attack that's performed with a combination of buttons, and when it lands, it deals tremendous damage. It can be used as a punishing tool if your opponent makes a mistake or leaves themselves open.
  - o **Power Geyser**: Another of Terry's powerful super moves, the **Power Geyser** is a long-range, high-damage attack that can be used to break through an opponent's defenses from a distance.

Strengths and Weaknesses

- **Strengths**:
  - o Terry is one of the most well-rounded characters in the game, with a strong offensive game and reliable defensive tools.
  - o Great at controlling space with his **Power Wave** and closing the gap quickly with **Burn Knuckle**.
  - o High damage output, especially with his Super Moves like **Buster Wolf** and **Power Geyser**.
- **Weaknesses**:

- While Terry has a versatile moveset, his attacks can sometimes be predictable if overused, especially his signature **Burn Knuckle** and **Power Wave**.
- His reliance on close-range combat makes him vulnerable to zoning characters who can keep him at a distance.

Strategic Tips for Terry

- **Control the Space**: Use **Power Wave** to control mid-range space and force your opponent to come to you. Once they do, you can follow up with quick, powerful attacks like **Burn Knuckle** or **Crack Shoot**.
- **Punish with Buster Wolf**: Always look for opportunities to land a **Buster Wolf**, especially when your opponent makes a mistake or leaves themselves vulnerable. It's a great move for punishing whiffs and slow attacks.
- **Close the Distance**: Terry excels in close-range combat, so use your special moves and quick attacks to keep the pressure on your opponent. **Rising Tackle** is especially useful for countering aerial opponents or punishing jump-ins.

Terry Bogard and Rock Howard are two of the most iconic characters in *Fatal Fury: City of the Wolves*, each with unique abilities, strengths, and weaknesses. Mastering their move sets and understanding their strategic advantages is essential for anyone looking to dominate the game. Whether you prefer Terry's powerful, hard-hitting style or Rock's balanced and versatile approach, both characters offer a deep and satisfying combat experience.

5.3 Mai Shiranui

Mai Shiranui is one of the most beloved and iconic characters in the *Fatal Fury* series. Known for her dazzling fighting style and her exuberant personality, Mai is a formidable opponent in *Fatal Fury: City of the Wolves*. Her agility, speed, and use of ninja techniques make her a unique and unpredictable fighter.

Backstory

- **Heritage and Training**: Mai is the granddaughter of the renowned ninja and martial arts master, Hanzo Shiranui. Trained in the Shiranui-ryu ninja style, she is adept at using fire-based techniques and relies on her incredible agility in combat. Mai is fiercely loyal to her family and often finds herself fighting alongside her allies in order to protect her loved ones, especially her mentor, Andy Bogard.
- **Personality**: Mai is playful, confident, and has a flirtatious side. While she often displays a cheerful and lighthearted demeanor, she is deadly serious in battle. Her devotion to her family and friends is unwavering, and she is always ready to defend those she cares about, especially her longtime crush, Andy.

Fighting Style

- **Ninja Agility and Fire Techniques**:
  Mai is highly agile and specializes in using her speed and acrobatic abilities to overwhelm her opponents. Her ninja training allows her to execute rapid, unpredictable movements, making her difficult to hit. Additionally, she

combines her agility with fire-based moves, creating a unique fighting style that's both flashy and dangerous.

- **Special Moves:**
  - **Kachū Tenshin Amaguriken**: Mai's signature move, the **Kachū Tenshin Amaguriken**, involves a rapid barrage of punches that are incredibly fast and difficult to block. This is her go-to move for putting pressure on her opponents and setting up for devastating combos.
  - **Shiranui-ryu Fireball**: Mai can summon a **fireball** by using her **Shiranui-ryu** techniques. It can be used as a zoning tool to control space and punish opponents who try to keep their distance.
  - **Tsubame Gaeshi**: This quick, spinning attack allows Mai to strike her opponent with a fast aerial move that can be used to either attack or evade. It's great for punishing opponents who are trying to close in on her.
  - **Mai's Whirlwind Kick**: A fast, spinning kick that Mai can use to control mid-range. It's highly effective for catching opponents off guard, especially after she's baited them into attacking.
- **Super Moves:**
  - **Phoenix Fire Dance**: Mai's **Phoenix Fire Dance** is one of her most devastating moves, where she unleashes a series of fiery attacks in quick succession. The speed and range of the move allow her to corner an opponent and deal significant damage if they aren't careful.
  - **Shiranui's Inferno**: A powerful and visually stunning super move where Mai engulfs her opponent in flames with a rapid barrage of fireballs and kicks. This move is perfect for punishing a cornered opponent or finishing a fight.

Strengths and Weaknesses

- **Strengths**:
  - Extremely fast and agile, allowing for quick hit-and-run tactics.
  - Great aerial mobility, with her ability to cancel her jumps into attacks.
  - Strong zoning abilities with her fireball moves and excellent combo potential.
- **Weaknesses**:
  - Mai relies heavily on her speed, and while she's agile, she can be vulnerable to more powerful, slower characters who can outlast her in a battle of attrition.
  - Her fire-based moves are effective but can be countered by characters with quick reflexes or those who specialize in deflecting projectiles.

Strategic Tips for Mai

- **Utilize Agility**: Mai thrives on movement. Make full use of her aerial abilities and quick footwork to stay unpredictable in combat. Keep your opponent guessing with a mix of ground and aerial attacks.
- **Control Space with Fireballs**: Use **Shiranui-ryu Fireball** to control space and limit your opponent's movement. This allows you to approach safely or bait out counter-attacks.
- **Pressure with Kachū Tenshin Amaguriken**: The **Kachū Tenshin Amaguriken** is a fast, multi-hit combo that's great for pressuring opponents. It's difficult to block, so don't hesitate to use it when you see an opening.
- **Use Super Moves Wisely**: Wait for the right moment to use **Phoenix Fire Dance** or **Shiranui's Inferno**. These

moves are powerful and can turn the tide of battle, but using them recklessly can leave you vulnerable.

5.4 Preecha and Other Notable Fighters

While the main characters like Rock Howard, Terry Bogard, and Mai Shiranui often take center stage, *Fatal Fury: City of the Wolves* also features a roster of notable fighters, including some new faces and old favorites who play key roles in the story and combat dynamics. These characters provide depth and variety to the roster, each with their own unique fighting styles and backstories.

Preecha

Preecha is a newly introduced character in *Fatal Fury: City of the Wolves* and serves as an important part of the expanded roster, bringing with him a fresh style and set of abilities that fit well into the game's dynamic combat system.

- **Backstory**:
  Preecha hails from a distant, war-torn kingdom where martial prowess is held in high esteem. He has spent years training in secret, mastering a blend of ancient combat techniques and newer, more brutal methods. Driven by a desire to prove himself on the world stage, Preecha enters the South Town tournament to challenge the best fighters and earn a place among the elite.
- **Fighting Style**:
  Preecha's fighting style is a mix of traditional martial arts and unorthodox moves that combine speed, power, and

agility. He's known for his unpredictable and aggressive approach, using rapid strikes and powerful grappling techniques.

- **Special Moves:**
    - Iron Fist Charge: A fast, charging punch that can break through an opponent's guard and send them staggering back. This move is great for closing the gap between you and a ranged fighter.
    - Skyward Takedown: Preecha's **Skyward Takedown** is a fast and vicious throw that can be used to close in on an opponent or punish them for attempting to block too much.
- **Super Move:**
    - Final Judgment: Preecha's **Final Judgment** is a devastating super move where he launches into a rapid series of attacks, finishing with a devastating knockout punch. The move has a large range and is highly damaging.

Other Notable Fighters

- **Andy Bogard:** The younger brother of Terry Bogard, Andy brings his unique style of **Atemi Karate** to the table. His moves are quick and precise, with a heavy emphasis on quick strikes and counter-attacks.
- **Joe Higashi:** A Muay Thai fighter known for his powerful, unrelenting kicks and tough endurance. Joe excels in close-range combat and can overwhelm opponents with his rapid strikes and explosive moves.
- **Geese Howard:** As one of the most iconic villains of the series, Geese Howard's return in *City of the Wolves* continues to challenge the protagonists. Known for his overwhelming strength and mastery of martial arts,

Geese's deadly counter-attacks and fast combos make him a formidable opponent.

- **Kim Kaphwan**: A martial artist from South Korea, Kim's style focuses on speed and precision, using rapid punches and kicks to overwhelm his opponents. His ability to chain moves together makes him an effective offensive fighter.
- **Mai Shiranui's Allies**: Characters like **Andy Bogard** and **Iori Yagami** also make appearances in *Fatal Fury: City of the Wolves*, each bringing their own distinctive fighting style and abilities to the game's diverse roster.

Strengths and Weaknesses of Other Fighters

- **Strengths**:
    - Characters like **Joe Higashi** and **Andy Bogard** excel in offense, with fast, devastating strikes and excellent combo potential.
    - **Geese Howard** is one of the most powerful characters, with brutal counter-attacks and devastating super moves.
    - **Kim Kaphwan** excels at maintaining pressure with speed, making him a strong choice for players who enjoy quick, rapid combat.
- **Weaknesses**:
    - Some of the lighter characters like **Andy Bogard** or **Mai Shiranui** may struggle against heavier, more defensive fighters who can absorb damage and push back.
    - Characters like **Joe Higashi** may be vulnerable to projectiles and zoning techniques, as his attacks are better suited for close-range combat.

Fatal Fury: City of the Wolves is filled with an eclectic mix of fighters, each contributing unique strengths to the game's roster.

From the fire-based agility of Mai Shiranui to the new challenger Preecha's deadly grappling techniques, every fighter brings their own dynamic to the battle. Understanding their strengths, weaknesses, and special moves will be key to mastering the game and dominating your opponents in South Town.

CHAPTER 6: UNLOCKABLES AND SECRETS

6.1 DLC Characters and Season Pass

In *Fatal Fury: City of the Wolves*, the post-launch content includes downloadable characters and additional content via the Season Pass, providing players with even more variety and gameplay options. These DLC characters and features help keep the game fresh, offering new fighting styles, backstories, and ways to interact with the game world.

DLC Characters

- **What Are DLC Characters?**
  DLC characters are additional fighters that are released after the game's initial launch, typically through digital downloads. These characters expand the roster and offer unique movesets, backstories, and storylines. Each DLC character is designed to bring new strategies and playstyles to the game, encouraging players to experiment with fresh approaches.
- **Available DLC Fighters**:
  - **Geese Howard (Alternate Costume)**: One of the most requested characters, Geese returns with an alternate costume and moveset that brings additional layers to his already dangerous playstyle.
  - **Mai Shiranui (New Outfit & Moves)**: A new version of Mai Shiranui, featuring a different set of special moves and enhanced animations that

showcase her agility and ninja techniques in new ways.

- **Eiji Kisaragi**: A renowned character from the *King of Fighters* series, Eiji brings his unique ninjutsu style, which can be used to overwhelm opponents with fast, deceptive attacks and defensive counters.
- **Billy Kane (Team Mode)**: Billy Kane, armed with his signature staff, is available as a DLC fighter with new combo opportunities and added flair to his heavy-hitting moves.

- **Unlocking DLC Fighters:**
These fighters are unlocked via the **Season Pass**, a bundle that grants access to a series of downloadable content for a discounted price compared to purchasing each DLC character individually. Players who own the Season Pass will have automatic access to all new characters as soon as they are released, and they can dive right into learning their unique moves and strategies.

- **Character Balance and Updates:**
DLC characters often come with their own unique balance adjustments to make them both fair and powerful in the game's ecosystem. Expect adjustments to the combat mechanics to ensure that these new additions don't disrupt the core gameplay, as well as fine-tuning to ensure each character is both fun to play and competitive.

Season Pass Overview

- **What's Included in the Season Pass?**
The Season Pass is a bundle that grants players access to all the post-launch content for a discounted price. This includes DLC characters, new costumes, and even new gameplay modes or features, such as additional story

content or expanded multiplayer options. The Season Pass allows players to get the most out of their purchase by unlocking content as soon as it is made available.

- **Benefits of the Season Pass**:
    - ○ **Immediate Access**: With the Season Pass, you won't have to wait for individual releases. Each new DLC character and content update is automatically available to you.
    - ○ **Exclusive Content**: Often, Season Pass holders get exclusive content that isn't available for individual purchase, such as special skins, alternate outfits, and exclusive in-game bonuses.
    - ○ **Cost Savings**: Purchasing the Season Pass is usually more cost-effective than buying each DLC character or content pack individually.
- **How to Purchase**:
  The Season Pass is available for purchase through the in-game store or external digital marketplaces like the PlayStation Store, Xbox Marketplace, or Steam, depending on your platform. Be sure to check for any seasonal promotions or bundles that might offer extra content for a limited time.

6.2 Hidden Stages and Arenas

One of the exciting features of *Fatal Fury: City of the Wolves* is its collection of **hidden stages** and **arenas**, which can add layers of depth to the gameplay experience. These hidden locations offer unique settings and challenges that aren't immediately available in the main game, but can be unlocked through specific actions or conditions.

What Are Hidden Stages?

Hidden stages are special battle arenas that are not accessible through the regular progression of the game. They require players to complete certain objectives, achieve high scores, or enter specific codes in order to unlock them. These stages often feature unique visual designs, soundtracks, and challenges, giving players fresh environments to fight in and enjoy.

How to Unlock Hidden Stages:

1. **Complete Specific Challenges**: Some hidden stages can be unlocked by completing in-game challenges, such as winning a certain number of battles with specific characters, achieving high ranks in different game modes, or completing certain objectives in story mode.
2. **Secret Combos or Actions**: In true *Fatal Fury* style, some stages are unlocked through hidden combos or input sequences. For example, performing a specific combination of moves at a certain point in the game might reveal a new arena to fight in.
3. **Unlockable via DLC or Season Pass**: Some hidden stages are tied to DLC content or the Season Pass. These may be tied to new characters, expanding the number of available arenas.

Notable Hidden Stages:

- **Geese Tower Rooftop**: A dangerous stage set atop the infamous Geese Tower, complete with dramatic lighting and an ever-present sense of danger. Fighters battle while the lights flicker and the rain falls, creating an intense atmosphere.

- **South Town Streets**: A more urban setting, featuring the gritty backstreets of South Town. Broken windows, abandoned cars, and graffiti-covered walls give this stage a unique aesthetic. Players can interact with elements in the environment for bonus points or special effects.
- **Shiranui Shrine**: This stage is a traditional Japanese temple surrounded by cherry blossoms, creating a stark contrast to the other darker, urban locations in the game. The peaceful yet deadly environment reflects Mai's ninja heritage, and players can unlock it by completing a series of combo challenges.
- **Underground Fight Club**: Hidden deep beneath South Town, this arena is used by underground fighters and crime syndicates. It's dimly lit with a cage-like atmosphere, offering a gritty and brutal vibe as combatants face off in an arena with limited escape routes.

Benefits of Hidden Stages:

- **Unique Visuals and Atmospheres**: Each hidden stage has its own aesthetic, ranging from traditional Japanese settings to dark urban environments. These stages keep the gameplay feeling fresh and offer players exciting new places to battle.
- **Environmental Interactions**: Some hidden stages include interactive elements that can affect gameplay. For example, environmental hazards like crumbling buildings, fireworks, or falling debris might disrupt a fight, creating unique challenges.
- **Unlockables**: Hidden stages often come with unique rewards, such as exclusive music tracks, background story elements, or even special items. These unlockables add

extra depth and incentive to find and explore hidden arenas.

Strategies for Unlocking Hidden Stages:

- **Explore Different Game Modes**: Hidden stages can sometimes be unlocked through specific game modes like **Arcade**, **Survival**, or **Team Battles**. Try different settings and objectives to see what might trigger new arenas to become available.
- **Replay Story Mode**: Certain hidden stages may appear after certain milestones in the game's storyline. Replay chapters or different routes to uncover new challenges and environments.
- **Check for Special Events**: Occasionally, limited-time events or special challenges in the game might unlock hidden stages. These events are often tied to seasonal updates, such as holiday-themed content or anniversary events.

6.3 Special Costumes and Customizations

In *Fatal Fury: City of the Wolves*, players have the opportunity to further personalize their experience through special costumes and customizations. These cosmetic changes offer a way to express individual style while also adding some fun and flair to the game. Whether through character skins, alternate outfits, or other visual customizations, players can enhance their experience by unlocking new looks for their favorite fighters.

What Are Special Costumes?

Special costumes are alternate outfits that alter the appearance of a character. These costumes may be inspired by the fighter's past appearances, alternate designs, or even pop-culture references. Some special costumes are purely aesthetic, while others may come with unique animations or effects that enhance the character's overall visual impact in battle.

How to Unlock Special Costumes:

1. **Achieving Milestones**: Some special costumes are unlocked by completing specific milestones in the game. This could involve reaching a certain level, completing all challenges in a particular game mode, or finishing the storyline with specific characters.
2. **DLC and Seasonal Events**: Many special costumes are available through downloadable content (DLC) or through limited-time events. For instance, holiday-themed costumes, anniversary skins, or collaborations with other games may be released as part of seasonal updates.
3. **In-Game Store Purchases**: Certain special costumes can be purchased directly through the in-game store or marketplaces on digital platforms like the PlayStation Store, Xbox Marketplace, or Steam. These costumes may be sold individually or as part of a larger bundle.
4. **Pre-order Bonuses or Exclusive Content**: Special outfits might also be available as part of a pre-order bonus or as exclusive content for those who supported the game early. These costumes are typically limited in availability and can be a way to show off your dedication to the game.

Popular Special Costumes:

- **Retro Skins**: These costumes give fighters a throwback look, inspired by their original appearances in earlier *Fatal Fury* or *King of Fighters* games. These skins often come with updated animations and effects while still capturing the essence of the character's classic design.
- **Holiday or Seasonal Outfits**: These costumes are often introduced during special holiday events such as Halloween, Christmas, or New Year's. Characters may wear themed outfits, like Terry Bogard in a Santa hat or Mai Shiranui in a Halloween costume.
- **Crossover Costumes**: *Fatal Fury: City of the Wolves* may include special costumes inspired by other games, movies, or franchises as part of collaborations. For instance, a character might sport an outfit referencing a famous movie or a legendary fighter from another SNK title.
- **Signature or Elite Costumes**: Elite costumes often represent special achievements or milestones, such as completing a high level of difficulty or achieving the highest rank in the game's online mode. These costumes are a symbol of your hard work and dedication.

Character Customization:

In addition to costumes, the game allows for a degree of customization in terms of character visuals, such as:

- **Color Palettes**: Change the color scheme of your fighter's clothing, hair, and other elements.
- **Alternate Accessories**: Unlock or customize accessories like belts, gloves, shoes, and even tattoos for your characters.

- **Battle Animations**: Some customizations include minor changes to battle animations, like a character performing an exclusive taunt or victory pose.

Benefits of Special Costumes and Customizations:

- **Personal Expression**: Special costumes and customizations allow you to express yourself and showcase your style within the game. They add a fun layer of personality to your fighter and the overall experience.
- **Visual Appeal**: New costumes and visual effects make the game feel fresh, allowing players to experience their favorite characters in new and exciting ways.
- **Unlockables and Rewards**: Many players enjoy the challenge of unlocking special costumes as they progress through the game. These unlockables serve as rewards for your efforts, adding an extra layer of motivation.

6.4 Achievements and Trophies

Achievements and trophies are integral to the *Fatal Fury: City of the Wolves* experience for players who enjoy challenging themselves and gaining recognition for their progress. These in-game accomplishments provide a sense of achievement and unlock special rewards, such as character skins, access to additional content, or bragging rights in the community.

What Are Achievements and Trophies?

Achievements and trophies are system-wide accomplishments that track a player's progress and accomplishments within the game. They can be earned by completing various tasks, such as defeating certain opponents, winning a set number of matches, mastering specific moves, or completing certain levels under specific conditions. These accomplishments are tied to a player's account, allowing for permanent tracking of progress and milestones.

Types of Achievements and Trophies:

1. **Story Mode Achievements**:
   - **Complete Story Mode**: Finish the main story with each character to earn an achievement or trophy. These typically come with a unique reward or unlockable, such as a new character skin or concept art.
   - **Unlock All Endings**: Some achievements are awarded for unlocking alternate story endings, which could involve completing the story in a specific way or choosing certain paths during narrative moments.
2. **Combat-Based Achievements**:
   - **Perfect Victory**: Achieve a flawless victory by defeating an opponent without taking any damage. This may seem difficult, but it's an essential challenge for skilled players looking to master the game.
   - **Combo Master**: Perform a specific number of successful combos in a single match. This trophy

rewards players who can execute advanced combat techniques.

3. **Character-Specific Achievements**:
   o **Character Mastery**: Each fighter has their own set of achievements. For example, achieving a certain number of wins with a character, performing all of their special moves in one match, or executing their super moves successfully.
   o **Unlock Character-Specific Challenges**: Some trophies require players to complete particular challenges with a specific fighter, like completing a set number of battles with Rock Howard or Terry Bogard.

4. **Online Multiplayer Achievements**:
   o **Ranked Champion**: Achieve a high rank in online multiplayer mode. This could be achieved by winning a series of ranked matches or reaching a specific level in online competition.
   o **Online Warrior**: Complete a certain number of online matches, whether you win or lose. This could also include achievements tied to unique online modes like tournaments or team-based battles.

5. **Miscellaneous Achievements**:
   o **Unlock All DLC Content**: For those who have purchased the DLC or the Season Pass, achievements are awarded for unlocking all the downloadable content, including new characters, costumes, and stages.
   o **Completionist**: Earned for completing all available in-game challenges and collecting all available trophies and achievements.

Trophy Rarity:

- **Bronze Trophies**: Typically awarded for simple tasks or for achieving early milestones in the game.
- **Silver Trophies**: These are generally for more difficult accomplishments, such as mastering harder game modes or completing challenging side objectives.
- **Gold Trophies**: The most prestigious trophies, often requiring expert-level gameplay or unlocking major achievements, such as completing the game on the hardest difficulty or winning a tournament.
- **Platinum Trophy**: The ultimate achievement in *Fatal Fury: City of the Wolves*, awarded to players who collect all other trophies in the game. It is a mark of a true completionist and shows dedication to mastering every aspect of the game.

Benefits of Achievements and Trophies:

- **Sense of Accomplishment**: Achievements provide players with a sense of satisfaction and progression, rewarding them for the time and effort spent mastering the game.
- **Replay Value**: Achievements encourage players to revisit the game and try different strategies, characters, and modes. Whether it's to unlock a hidden achievement or complete a difficult task, these milestones offer additional incentives to keep playing.
- **Leaderboards and Community Recognition**: Trophies can also be a form of bragging rights, showing off your achievements to the community, whether through online leaderboards or social media sharing.

CHAPTER 7: ONLINE PLAY AND COMMUNITY ENGAGEMENT

7.1 Setting Up Online Matches

Online multiplayer is one of the key features of *Fatal Fury: City of the Wolves*, allowing players to compete against others from around the world. Whether you're a seasoned fighter or a newcomer, setting up online matches is easy and straightforward, ensuring a seamless experience in both casual and competitive settings.

How to Set Up an Online Match:

1. **Access the Online Menu**:
   From the main menu, select the "Online" tab to enter the online multiplayer interface. This section provides all the options necessary to connect with other players, including casual matches, ranked matches, and custom lobbies.
2. **Choosing Match Type**:
   - **Casual Matches**: Casual online matches allow you to play for fun without the pressure of rankings or competitive points. These matches are perfect for practice, testing new characters, or simply enjoying a laid-back game with others.
   - **Ranked Matches**: In ranked matches, every win or loss counts toward your overall ranking. This is where competitive players can challenge each other and climb the leaderboards.
   - **Custom Lobbies**: For those looking for a more personalized experience, custom lobbies allow you to create your own online match, invite friends,

set specific rules, and adjust settings such as time limits and stages.

3. **Finding an Opponent**:
   o **Quick Match**: If you're looking to jump into a match quickly, select the "Quick Match" option. The game will automatically pair you with an opponent of similar skill based on the matchmaking system.
   o **Friend Matches**: If you want to play with a friend, you can invite them to your match or join their session through the "Friend Match" option. You can send invites directly via your platform's friend system, whether it's PlayStation, Xbox, or Steam.

4. **Match Settings**:
   Before starting an online match, you may need to select your preferred rules:
   o **Time Limit**: Choose how long the match will last. Options generally range from 30 seconds to several minutes, depending on your preference.
   o **Number of Rounds**: Decide whether you want to play a single round or multiple rounds to determine the winner.
   o **Stage Selection**: Some online modes allow players to pick the stage they want to fight on, while others might have random stage selection enabled.

5. **Ready Up**:
   Once you and your opponent have selected your characters and agreed on the settings, both players will need to "ready up" to confirm they're ready to start the match. This step ensures that no one is caught off guard by sudden changes.

6. **In-Game Communication**:
   Online matches often include communication options

such as text chat, emotes, or voice chat (if enabled). This is particularly useful for coordinating with friends or just enjoying the social aspect of online play.

Online Match Etiquette:

- **Respecting Opponents**: Always maintain sportsmanship and respect during online matches. Avoid trash-talking or engaging in any disruptive behavior that can negatively impact the enjoyment of the game for others.
- **No Cheating or Exploiting**: The game has mechanisms to detect cheating or exploiting glitches. Fair play is key to maintaining a healthy online community.
- **Connection Stability**: Ensure your internet connection is stable for smooth gameplay. Lag can heavily impact your experience, so a wired connection is recommended for optimal performance.

7.2 Understanding Matchmaking and Rankings

Matchmaking and rankings are integral parts of the online multiplayer experience in *Fatal Fury: City of the Wolves*. The game's system is designed to create fair, balanced matches, providing players with a competitive and rewarding experience as they rise through the ranks.

How Matchmaking Works:

1. **Skill-Based Matchmaking (SBMM)**:
   The game uses a **skill-based matchmaking** system to pair players of similar skill levels. The matchmaking algorithm takes into account your win/loss record, performance in

previous matches, and ranking points to find an opponent who is likely to provide a balanced and competitive fight. This ensures that new players aren't paired with experienced veterans, and experienced players aren't facing off against beginners who don't stand a chance.

2. **Finding Your First Match**:
   If you're a new player, you may start in a lower skill bracket, with easy-to-understand opponents to help you learn the mechanics. As you win matches and complete online battles, your matchmaking ranking will rise, and you'll start facing more challenging opponents.

3. **Factors Affecting Matchmaking**:
   - **Ranking Level**: Players are matched based on their rankings, so you'll face opponents in the same rank, ensuring that your skill levels are close.
   - **Connection Quality**: The game also takes your connection quality into account. If your ping is too high or unstable, you may be paired with other players who have similar connection speeds to minimize lag and ensure a smooth gameplay experience.
   - **Region**: Players from the same or nearby regions are often matched together to improve connection stability and reduce latency.

4. **Fairness and Balance**:
   While matchmaking strives to create balanced matches, occasional mismatches can occur, especially if you're playing at times with fewer players online. In this case, the game may widen the matchmaking range to find a match, but it will still aim for fairness by considering other factors like win rates and combat performance.

Understanding the Ranking System:

The ranking system provides players with a sense of progression, rewarding them for victories and incentivizing continuous improvement. As you compete in ranked matches, your rank will rise or fall based on your performance.

1. **Ranks and Tiers**:
   Players start at the **Bronze** tier and can climb up to **Silver**, **Gold**, **Platinum**, and ultimately to **Diamond** or **Master** ranks, depending on their skill level. Each rank has multiple divisions, with higher divisions representing more skilled players.
   - **Bronze**: Beginners, players who are just starting their journey.
   - **Silver**: Players who are grasping the mechanics and learning strategies.
   - **Gold**: More experienced players who have honed their skills.
   - **Platinum and Beyond**: Top-tier players who have mastered the game and perform at an elite level.
2. **Ranking Points (RP)**:
   After each match, you will gain or lose ranking points based on your performance. Winning a match against an opponent of a similar rank will reward you with a modest amount of points, while beating an opponent of a higher rank grants more points. Losing to an opponent with a lower rank will cost you points, but losing to someone with a higher rank will result in fewer points lost.
3. **Promotions and Relegations**:
   - **Promotion**: Winning enough matches in your current division will lead to a promotion to the next rank, unlocking access to tougher competition and higher-tier rewards.

- Relegation: Losing too many matches will cause you to be demoted to a lower rank. To avoid this, you need to consistently perform well and maintain a positive win rate.
4. **Leaderboards**:
   - **Global Rankings**: The global leaderboard shows the best players in the world, giving recognition to those who have reached the highest levels. Climbing the leaderboard requires consistent performance and a lot of dedication.
   - **Regional Leaderboards**: In addition to the global leaderboard, there may also be regional leaderboards based on your geographical location. Competing for top spots in your region can also bring local bragging rights and recognition.

Ranked Rewards:

- **Seasonal Rewards**: Some online ranking systems offer rewards at the end of each season. Players who finish in higher ranks may receive exclusive rewards such as rare costumes, character skins, or ranking-specific titles.
- **Exclusive Titles**: Higher-ranking players may earn special titles that are displayed beside their name during online matches, signifying their skill level and experience.
- **Ranking Points for Special Unlocks**: Ranking points can also contribute toward unlocking special content, such as exclusive stages, costumes, or character variants.

7.3 Participating in Tournaments

Tournaments are an exciting and competitive aspect of *Fatal Fury: City of the Wolves*, allowing players to compete against the best and showcase their skills in high-stakes, organized events. Whether local or global, tournaments provide a structured and thrilling environment for players looking to test their mettle against the finest fighters in the game.

How to Participate in Tournaments:

1. **Accessing Tournament Mode**:
   To enter tournaments, you can navigate to the "Tournaments" tab in the online menu. This is where all upcoming and ongoing tournaments are listed. Depending on the type of tournament (local, regional, or global), you can choose the one that best suits your schedule and level of experience.
2. **Registration**:
   Tournaments typically require players to register in advance. This can be done directly through the in-game interface. Once you select a tournament, you'll be asked to confirm your participation. Some tournaments may require an entry fee, while others are free to enter. Make sure to check the registration deadlines to avoid missing out.
3. **Types of Tournaments**:
   o **Open Tournaments**: These tournaments are available for all players, regardless of rank or experience. Open tournaments offer a great way to practice, improve, and compete with a wide range of players.

- Ranked Tournaments: Ranked tournaments often feature higher-level competitors and offer greater rewards, such as exclusive character skins, ranking points, or in-game currency.
- **Invitational Tournaments**: These are special, invite-only events that feature the top players in the game. Invitations are often extended to players who have demonstrated exceptional skill in ranked play or previous tournaments.

4. **Tournament Rules and Structure**:
   Each tournament has its own set of rules and structure. Common formats include:
   - **Single-Elimination**: Players compete in a knockout format, where each loss results in elimination from the tournament.
   - **Double-Elimination**: A more forgiving format, where players are given a second chance after losing one match. You'll need to lose two matches before being eliminated.
   - **Round Robin**: Each player faces every other player in the tournament, and the competitor with the best overall record is declared the winner.

5. **Match Settings**:
   Tournament matches often have specific rules and settings, such as time limits, number of rounds, or stage selection. The tournament organizers will inform you of these details before the event starts. Be sure to review and adjust your strategies according to the tournament's parameters.

Tournament Rewards:

1. **Exclusive Skins and Titles**:
   Winners and high-ranking players often receive special

rewards such as exclusive character skins, unique outfits, or in-game titles that signify their accomplishments in the tournament.

2. **Cash Prizes**:
Competitive tournaments, especially those at the professional or esports level, may offer cash prizes for top performers. These tournaments are often sponsored by major organizations and can lead to significant financial rewards for players.

3. **Leaderboard Placement**:
Successful tournament participants can also earn spots on global or regional leaderboards, gaining recognition as top players. Many tournaments contribute to players' overall online rankings, giving you a chance to boost your rank.

4. **In-Game Currency**:
Players who perform well in tournaments can earn in-game currency, which can be used to unlock characters, costumes, or other content within the game.

Tournament Etiquette:

- **Fair Play**: Just like in regular online matches, tournament matches require good sportsmanship. Respect your opponents, avoid cheating, and follow the rules of the event.
- **Prepare for Connectivity Issues**: Sometimes, connection problems can arise during online tournaments. Ensure your internet connection is stable, and be ready to deal with any technical issues promptly by following tournament organizers' guidelines.

Joining Major Esports Tournaments:

For the most serious players, *Fatal Fury: City of the Wolves* offers the opportunity to compete in professional esports tournaments. These events are broadcast live, often feature commentary, and attract large audiences, making them a great platform for showcasing high-level gameplay. Keep an eye on major tournament announcements to qualify and compete for bigger rewards.

7.4 Connecting with the Community

The *Fatal Fury* community is an essential part of the game's experience, and connecting with fellow players can enhance your enjoyment of the game. Whether you're looking for tips, joining online discussions, or forming teams to take on challenges together, the community is a fantastic resource for players.

Ways to Connect with the Community:

1. **Official Forums and Social Media**:
   - **Game Forums**: The *Fatal Fury: City of the Wolves* official forums provide a place for players to engage in discussions, share strategies, and provide feedback. You can find help with game mechanics, discuss tournament results, and even participate in community events.
   - **Social Media**: Follow the official *Fatal Fury* social media accounts on platforms like Twitter, Facebook, Instagram, and YouTube. These channels provide updates on new content,

upcoming tournaments, and other community events.

- o **Hashtags and Community Tags**: Use game-specific hashtags like #CityOfTheWolves and #FatalFuryCommunity on platforms like Twitter and Instagram to join conversations, share fan art, or find others with similar interests.

2. **Discord Servers**:

Many communities have dedicated **Discord servers** where players can chat in real-time, organize matches, and discuss strategies. Joining the *Fatal Fury* Discord can help you find teammates, participate in community events, and get advice from veteran players. Many servers also have voice channels for coordination during multiplayer matches.

3. **Fan-Created Content**:
   - o **Fan Art and Music**: The community is filled with creative individuals who create fan art, remixes of the game's music, or fan fiction based on the *Fatal Fury* universe. Sharing and discovering this content helps foster a deeper connection with the game.
   - o **Tutorials and Guides**: Many players in the community create tutorials and guides to help others improve their skills. Whether it's a combo guide, character breakdown, or strategy video, these resources are invaluable for newcomers and experienced players alike.

4. **Collaborations with Streamers and YouTubers**:
   - o **Streaming Platforms**: Platforms like Twitch and YouTube are excellent ways to engage with the *Fatal Fury* community. Many content creators specialize in fighting games and regularly stream tournaments, competitive play, or general

gameplay. You can learn new techniques, follow events, and even get tips from pro players.

- ○ **Community Challenges**: Streamers and YouTubers may organize community challenges, where viewers can compete against the streamer or other community members. Participating in these challenges can lead to recognition, fun rewards, or simply a great time with fellow players.

Participating in Community Events:

1. **Weekly or Monthly Tournaments**:
   Many fan-driven communities hold regular online tournaments that players can participate in for fun and prizes. These events are often open to all skill levels and allow for friendly competition. Keep an eye out for announcements from community organizers.

2. **Charity Events**:
   The *Fatal Fury* community often comes together for charity events, where players can donate to good causes while competing in special tournaments. These events may feature unique challenges or special rules to encourage participation.

3. **Collaborative Gameplay**:
   Join online communities that host collaborative gameplay sessions. Whether it's co-op matches, team-based battles, or simply hanging out and chatting, these events help strengthen the bonds between players and provide a more enjoyable and social experience.

Building Friendships and Finding Teammates:

- **Create or Join a Clan**: Many competitive players join or form clans within the community. These groups can help you find teammates for team-based events, share strategies, and practice regularly with like-minded players.

- **Local Meetups**: Some communities host local meetups and live events where players can gather, participate in local tournaments, and bond over shared interests in the game.

CHAPTER 8: TIPS AND STRATEGIES

8.1 Beginner's Guide to Combat

Combat in *Fatal Fury: City of the Wolves* is dynamic and requires a balance of strategy, timing, and skill. As a beginner, it's important to get a strong grasp of the fundamentals before diving into more complex techniques. This chapter will walk you through the basics of combat, helping you understand the core mechanics and giving you a solid foundation to build upon.

Core Combat Mechanics:

1. **Movement Basics**:
   - **Walking and Dashing**: Use the directional inputs to move your character around the screen. Walking is a slower form of movement, while dashing (by quickly tapping the direction) lets you move faster and can be used to close gaps or retreat from an opponent.
   - **Jumping and Air Control**: Jumping is essential for both attacking and evading. Use the jump button to leap over attacks, but also practice controlling your air movement. Some characters can perform unique aerial attacks that can catch opponents off guard.
   - **Blocking**: To block, simply hold back on the joystick or d-pad. Proper blocking is key to defense, especially against opponents with strong rush-down tactics. Timing your blocks to anticipate enemy attacks is crucial to minimizing damage.
2. **Basic Attacks**:

- **Light and Heavy Attacks**: Each character has a variety of light (quick) and heavy (strong) attacks. Light attacks are faster but deal less damage, while heavy attacks are slower but inflict more damage. Learn how to chain light attacks into heavier ones for effective combos.
- **Special Moves**: Every character has special moves that often require a combination of directional inputs and buttons. These moves can be crucial for punishing opponents, breaking their defense, or setting up combos. Practice executing these moves consistently in training mode.
- **Throws**: Throws are useful for closing distance or escaping an opponent's pressure. Pressing a specific combination of buttons can allow you to grab your opponent, deal damage, and potentially throw them into a disadvantageous position.

3. **Using Super Moves and EX Moves**:
   - **Super Moves**: Each character has a devastating super move that can be performed once their super meter is filled. Learning how to time and execute these moves effectively is essential for high-level play. These moves often require precise inputs but can deal massive damage and turn the tide of battle.
   - **EX Moves**: EX moves are enhanced versions of normal special moves that consume part of your meter. These attacks are more powerful, have added properties (such as invincibility frames), and can be the key to breaking through your opponent's defense.

4. **Essential Tactics**:
   - **Spacing and Footsies**: Maintaining proper distance between you and your opponent is crucial. In

footsies, you'll use quick attacks to poke at your opponent from a safe range and bait them into making mistakes, allowing you to punish them.

- o **Anti-Airs**: If your opponent tries to jump in on you, having an anti-air attack is vital. Learn your character's aerial defense options (like upward special moves or quick jumping attacks) to stop them from getting free hits.

Training Tips for Beginners:

- **Practice Simple Combos**: Start by practicing basic, easy-to-execute combos. They don't need to be complex, but learning to string together light and heavy attacks will form the core of your offensive strategy.
- **Master the Timing of Super Moves**: Practice filling your super meter and timing your super moves. These attacks can be game-changers, and knowing when and how to use them can provide significant advantage in tight situations.
- **Use the Training Mode**: The training mode is your best friend as a beginner. Here, you can practice moves and combos without the pressure of fighting a real opponent. Take your time to learn each character's moveset and practice defending against various attacks.

8.2 Advanced Techniques and Combos

As you become more comfortable with the basics of combat, it's time to dive into advanced techniques that will elevate your gameplay. Mastering these advanced techniques requires precise execution, quick reflexes, and a deeper understanding of the game's mechanics.

Advanced Techniques:

1. **Counter-Hitting and Punishes**:
   - **Counter-Hitting**: This is a technique where you perform an attack while your opponent is executing a move, interrupting their animation and causing them to be hit. Timing is crucial here—if you anticipate your opponent's actions correctly, you can punish their mistakes and deal significant damage.
   - **Punish Moves**: Certain attacks leave opponents vulnerable after they miss or block them. Identifying these "punishable" moments is key to gaining an advantage. Use fast moves or supers to punish these openings before your opponent has a chance to recover.
2. **Juggle Combos**:
   - **Juggling**: Juggling refers to hitting your opponent while they are in the air, unable to defend themselves. This technique is useful after launching an opponent with a special move or jump attack. Mastering juggle combos will allow you to maximize your damage output and keep your opponent in a constant state of vulnerability.
   - **Juggle Combos in the Corner**: The corner is a critical area of the screen. Once your opponent is cornered, you can set up long, damaging juggle combos. Learn how to maintain pressure and use special moves or EX moves to keep your opponent in the corner, preventing their escape.
3. **Frame Traps and Pressure**:

- **Frame Advantage**: Every move in *Fatal Fury: City of the Wolves* has a startup time, active frames, and recovery time. Knowing which of your attacks give you frame advantage (meaning you can act faster than your opponent after executing a move) can help you apply pressure and prevent them from escaping or countering.
- **Pressure Sequences**: In advanced play, it's common to use a series of fast, hard-to-block moves (also known as a "block string") to keep your opponent locked down. Mastering these sequences allows you to dictate the flow of battle and create openings for throws or special moves.

4. **Air Dash and Air Combos**:
   - **Air Dashing**: Some characters have the ability to dash through the air, allowing for greater mobility and the ability to pressure opponents in new ways. Air dashes can confuse your opponent and open them up for aerial combos or mix-ups.
   - **Air Combos**: Advanced players can string together attacks in the air. These combos usually require fast timing and a good understanding of your character's aerial capabilities. Mastering air-to-air combat allows you to keep the pressure on and deal substantial damage when your opponent is jumping.

5. **Mix-Ups and Mind Games**:
   - **Mix-Up Tactics**: A mix-up is a strategy designed to confuse your opponent by alternating between different attacks and actions. For example, you may alternate between throws, high/low attacks, or overheads to make it difficult for your opponent to predict your next move.

- **Mind Games**: These are psychological tactics where you attempt to trick your opponent into making mistakes or reacting incorrectly. By using fake-outs, delayed attacks, or baiting their counters, you can create opportunities to land big hits or set up devastating combos.

Advanced Combos:

1. **Metered Combos (EX and Super Moves)**:
   - **EX Combos**: Combining EX special moves into combos is one of the most powerful ways to deal damage. These moves are enhanced versions of your standard attacks and can juggle, knock down, or inflict more damage. Be sure to use your EX meter wisely, as it is limited.
   - **Super Combos**: After you build up your super meter, incorporating super moves into your combo strings can deliver massive damage. Experiment with timing your super moves after a combo to maximize damage while preventing your opponent from escaping.
2. **Counter-Comboing**:
   - **Counter-Comboing** is a technique where you reverse the momentum of a combo and use it against your opponent. For example, if your opponent is performing a combo, you can sometimes interrupt it with a counter move that allows you to continue your own combo instead.
3. **Corner Combo Strategies**:
   - **Cornering Your Opponent**: The corner is an excellent place to perform extended combos, especially for characters who can continue attacks after knocking an opponent down. When your

opponent is cornered, you can trap them with pressure tactics and juggle combos that they have no escape from. This can result in some of the highest damage outputs in the game.

Training Tips for Advanced Players:

- **Frame Data Study**: Advanced players often study the frame data of moves to understand which are safe on block, which can be punished, and which provide the best opportunities for combo extensions. This knowledge is key to gaining an edge in competitive matches.
- **Practice Reaction Speed**: Advanced techniques like counter-hitting and punishing require quick reflexes. To improve your reaction time, train in practice mode against different attack sequences and learn to react to your opponent's moves in real-time.
- **Experiment with Mix-Ups**: To keep your opponent guessing, use mix-up strategies during combos. Try different timings and attack variations to create confusion and openings for throws or high-damage moves.
- **Use Combo Trials**: Many characters come with combo trials in training mode, where you can learn and perfect their most advanced and damaging combos. These trials provide a step-by-step guide to mastering complex combo chains.

8.3 Countering Different Fighting Styles

In *Fatal Fury: City of the Wolves*, each character brings their own unique fighting style, which means that every match can feel like a different challenge. Mastering how to counter different fighting styles is essential for adapting to your opponents and gaining an upper hand in battle. Understanding the strengths and weaknesses of various playstyles can help you anticipate moves and create openings for punishing attacks.

Fighting Style Breakdown:

1. **Rushdown Fighters**:
   - **Characteristics**: Rushdown fighters are aggressive and excel at staying in close range, applying constant pressure to their opponents. They often rely on quick, relentless attacks to force mistakes and open up opportunities for combos.
   - **How to Counter**:
     - **Keep Distance**: Rushdown fighters rely on being close to you. Maintain a safe distance using pokes, projectiles, and long-range attacks to keep them from getting too close.
     - **Defensive Play**: Use blocking, backdashing, and counter-hitting to stop their pressure. Be ready to break their momentum with a well-timed throw or reversal.
     - **Punish Predictability**: Rushdown players may rely on repetitive attack patterns. Learn to predict their actions and punish unsafe moves with fast counter-attacks or super moves.
2. **Zoners**:
   - **Characteristics**: Zoners focus on controlling space by using long-range projectiles, keeping opponents at a distance. They often rely on controlling the pace of the match with their ability to poke from afar.

- o **How to Counter:**
  - **Close the Distance**: The key to beating zoners is to get in close. Use dashes, jumps, and evasion techniques to bypass their projectiles and close the gap.
  - **Projectiles of Your Own**: If your character has strong projectile moves, use them to challenge the zoner's range. Learn the spacing and timing of their projectiles to counter them with your own.
  - **Punish Mistimed Projectiles**: Zoners can be vulnerable when they miss a projectile or when they are recovering from one. Use fast, invincible moves (such as EX moves) to punish their attempts to zone.

3. **Defensive Fighters:**
   - o **Characteristics**: Defensive fighters are built to absorb and evade damage, often using block strings, counters, and excellent movement to wait for their opponent to make a mistake. They are typically patient and wait for an opening.
   - o **How to Counter:**
     - **Don't Overcommit**: Defensive players often capitalize on your mistakes. Don't throw out too many unsafe or predictable moves. Take your time and work your way in with measured attacks.
     - **Mix Up Your Approach**: Use a variety of attack angles and speeds. Change up your strategies with high/low attacks, grabs, and quick jump-ins to disrupt their defensive rhythm.
     - **Pressure and Interrupt**: Once you get close, apply pressure with throws,

overheads, or fast attack strings to break their defensive stance. Be mindful that some defensive fighters are great at countering attacks with reversals or block-cancels.

4. **Grapplers**:
   o **Characteristics**: Grapplers rely on powerful throws and close-range combat. Their strength lies in their ability to grab and deal massive damage when they get in close, often forcing you into uncomfortable situations.
   o **How to Counter**:
     ▪ **Stay Mobile**: Grapplers are dangerous when they get close, so always be on the move. Use jumping, dashing, and spacing to avoid being grabbed.
     ▪ **Use Projectiles and Pokes**: Grapplers struggle against long-range attacks. Keep your distance with projectiles, pokes, or fast sweep moves, and make sure to punish any failed attempts to approach.
     ▪ **Watch for Grab Attempts**: Be aware of the timing and spacing when dealing with grapplers. If they're using a grab-heavy strategy, anticipate their grabs and use quick escape techniques or jumping attacks to avoid them.

5. **Hybrid Fighters**:
   o **Characteristics**: Hybrid fighters blend aspects of other fighting styles, often switching between offensive and defensive strategies. They are versatile and can adapt to their opponents during a match.
   o **How to Counter**:

- **Adapt Your Strategy**: The key to countering hybrid fighters is to be equally adaptable. Pay attention to their playstyle and respond accordingly. If they go aggressive, switch to a defensive style; if they go defensive, apply pressure and force them to make a mistake.
- **Study Their Transitions**: Hybrid players will frequently switch between aggressive and defensive stances. Recognize these transitions and punish them when they commit to one playstyle too heavily.
- **Disrupt Their Rhythm**: Hybrid fighters can be tricky, so it's important to disrupt their rhythm with sudden changes in attack speed, timing, or movement.

General Tips for Countering Fighting Styles:

- **Be Patient**: Sometimes, the best way to counter a particular fighting style is to wait for your opponent to make a mistake. Patience and reading your opponent's actions are key.
- **Know Your Character's Strengths**: Understand your character's capabilities and how they can handle various fighting styles. Whether it's superior mobility, projectiles, or counters, play to your strengths and keep your opponent guessing.
- **Learn the Matchup**: Every character has strengths and weaknesses. Study the matchups to know which fighting styles your character excels at countering and which require more effort.

8.4 Surviving in Episodes of South Town

"Episodes of South Town" is one of the more challenging game modes in *Fatal Fury: City of the Wolves*, where players are tasked with surviving a series of increasingly difficult battles. This mode challenges your endurance, requiring you to fight against multiple waves of enemies while managing health, resources, and strategy. Here's how to not only survive but thrive in the "Episodes of South Town."

Understanding the Episodes Mode:

1. **Structure of the Mode**:
   o **Waves of Enemies**: The Episodes mode is divided into several waves, each featuring different sets of enemies with varying difficulty. Each wave increases in complexity, often introducing new fighters or more aggressive tactics from your opponents.
   o **Boss Fights**: At the end of certain episodes, you'll face off against powerful bosses. These fights require special attention to patterns and can test your understanding of the game's mechanics.
2. **Resource Management**:
   o **Health Management**: You won't be able to heal between waves in Episodes of South Town, so managing your health across multiple fights is key. Use defensive tactics, blocks, and careful evasion to minimize damage during battles.
   o **Meter Management**: Your special move and super meter are limited. Be strategic about when you use your EX moves or supers. Using them too early

or too often may leave you without the power needed to deal with tougher waves or bosses.

- o **Item Pickups**: Some waves will have items that can restore health or give you an advantage, such as power-ups that increase attack damage or speed. Keep an eye out for these items, but don't risk your life just to grab them.

Survival Tactics:

1. **Adapt to Enemy Patterns**:
   - o Each wave and opponent in Episodes of South Town has specific attack patterns. Learning these patterns is essential for surviving long enough to progress. Pay attention to the timing of enemy attacks and use blocking, evasion, and counter-hitting to minimize damage.
   - o **Take Advantage of Weaknesses**: Every enemy has weaknesses that you can exploit. For example, some enemies may have slow recovery after certain attacks, leaving them vulnerable to combo punishments. Learn the vulnerabilities of each wave's fighters to maximize your damage output.

2. **Positioning**:
   - o **Control the Space**: Positioning is critical in Episodes of South Town. Always be mindful of your location relative to the enemy. If you find yourself cornered, it can be much harder to evade or block attacks.
   - o **Avoid Corners**: Being trapped in a corner leaves you with limited escape options, especially when facing multiple enemies. Stay mobile and move around the stage to keep your options open. Use dashes or quick jumps to escape tight situations.

3. **Boss Strategies**:
   - **Study Boss Mechanics**: Bosses in Episodes of South Town often have unique mechanics and devastating attacks. Take your time learning their move sets, especially their most powerful attacks, so you can anticipate them and avoid damage.
   - **Punish Boss Vulnerabilities**: Bosses usually have windows of opportunity where they are vulnerable. During these moments, you should unleash your most powerful combos or supers to deal massive damage. Focus on these windows rather than trying to chip away at the boss's health during every phase of the fight.
4. **Staying Calm Under Pressure**:
   - **Don't Panic**: As the waves increase in difficulty, it can be easy to panic and start making mistakes. Stay calm, focus on your enemy's movements, and remember your training. Panicking leads to unnecessary damage and missed opportunities.
   - **Focus on One Enemy at a Time**: If fighting multiple enemies, it's best to focus on one at a time. Take out weaker enemies first, if possible, to reduce the number of threats on screen.

Tips for High Scores and Completion:

1. **Use Continues Wisely**: If you're struggling to get through a wave, it's tempting to use continues, but using them recklessly can lead to running out of resources. Save your continues for the toughest situations or bosses.
2. **Aim for Combos and Perfects**: Doing long combos or finishing off enemies without taking damage is key to scoring high in Episodes of South Town. Perfect runs will reward you with higher points and additional bonuses.

3. **Know When to Play Safe**: In some waves, playing too aggressively can be your downfall. Be patient, observe your enemies' movements, and only strike when it's safe to do so.

CHAPTER 9: POST-LAUNCH UPDATES AND FUTURE CONTENT

9.1 Upcoming DLC Fighters

One of the exciting aspects of *Fatal Fury: City of the Wolves* is the promise of downloadable content (DLC), which continues to expand the roster and features of the game. With each new DLC fighter, players can expect new playstyles, movesets, and stories that add variety and depth to the game.

Introduction to DLC Fighters:

- DLC fighters typically bring unique abilities and playstyles to the game, adding new dynamics to both the roster and combat mechanics. These new characters often come with fresh storylines and interactions, which can affect the overarching narrative of *City of the Wolves*.

Expected DLC Fighters:

1. **Character Reveals**:
   - **Teasers and Leaks**: Throughout the game's life cycle, teasers and leaks will reveal potential fighters coming in future DLC updates. Players can expect characters who either have rich histories within the *Fatal Fury* universe or new characters designed specifically for *City of the Wolves*.
   - **Classic Fighters**: Many *Fatal Fury* veterans like Geese Howard, Andy Bogard, or even lesser-known characters may make their return. Expect

their move sets to be expanded or refined to fit the new game mechanics.

- **Brand New Faces**: New fighters are expected to be introduced, including original characters created for this installment of *Fatal Fury*. These characters will have their own unique backstories and fighting styles, offering fresh challenges for players.

2. **Character Abilities and Styles**:
   - Each DLC fighter will have distinct abilities, special moves, and super moves that reflect their personality and fighting background. Some may have traditional styles, while others may bring more creative or experimental mechanics to the table.
   - The development team will likely add a mix of characters with both close-range and long-range abilities, giving players more options to find their preferred playstyle.

3. **Storyline Integration**:
   - New DLC fighters will be integrated into the story, either through personal storylines or larger narrative arcs. Players can expect new interactions with existing characters, adding layers to the plot and further developing the *Fatal Fury* universe.

How to Unlock and Access DLC Fighters:

- DLC fighters will be accessible through various methods: either purchased separately, included as part of the Season Pass, or unlocked through in-game challenges or milestones.

9.2 Season Pass Details

The *City of the Wolves* Season Pass offers players a way to access a variety of content updates over time. This includes additional fighters, costumes, stages, and other in-game bonuses. The Season Pass is designed to enhance the longevity of the game by delivering consistent new content and updates.

Overview of the Season Pass:

1. **What's Included**:
   - **DLC Fighters**: The Season Pass guarantees access to upcoming DLC fighters as they are released. Players who purchase the Season Pass will get early access to these new characters and often receive exclusive fighters before they are made available for individual purchase.
   - **Exclusive Costumes and Skins**: Along with fighters, the Season Pass may include special costumes, skins, or alternate appearances for existing characters. These can be purely cosmetic but allow for personalization and new ways to experience the game.
   - **New Stages**: Expect new, exciting arenas or stages for your fighters to battle on, each with its own unique environment and hazards that impact the flow of the match.
2. **Season Pass Tiers**:
   - **Standard Pass**: The base Season Pass typically includes a selection of DLC fighters, stages, and costumes. It provides great value for players who want access to a good chunk of the game's post-launch content.

- Ultimate Pass: The more expensive option might include all DLC content plus special bonuses such as exclusive skins, early access to new characters, or behind-the-scenes content. Some bundles might also feature limited-time cosmetics or skins.

3. **Pricing and Availability**:
   - The price of the Season Pass will vary depending on the number of included DLC packs. Season Passes can typically be purchased through the game's store, either in-game or via external platforms, depending on where you're playing.

4. **When the Content Drops**:
   - Players will receive content from the Season Pass in a scheduled release, often one or two major updates per season. The exact release schedule can vary, with larger updates coming every few months and smaller, incremental updates released more regularly.

9.3 Community Feedback and Developer Responses

The *Fatal Fury: City of the Wolves* community plays a vital role in the game's continued development. Developers pay close attention to fan feedback, adjusting gameplay, fixing bugs, and implementing features based on the input from players. Here's how the community feedback loop functions:

How Feedback Shapes the Game:

1. **Listening to Players**:

- Developers actively monitor online forums, social media platforms, and in-game feedback systems to collect player opinions, suggestions, and complaints. Popular forums like Reddit, Discord, and official game sites allow players to voice their concerns and share their experiences.
- Players often report issues with balance, gameplay mechanics, or character interactions, which developers then address in future patches or updates.

2. **Developer Responses**:
   - Developers are often very transparent about the changes they make based on feedback. If a certain character is deemed overpowered or underperforming, the developers may issue a balance update to fix these issues. Similarly, bug fixes, quality-of-life improvements, or gameplay enhancements often come directly from community input.
   - In some cases, developers might hold Q&A sessions, livestreams, or polls where players can directly influence future updates or even suggest new characters, features, or design changes.

3. **Community Events and Involvement**:
   - Many developers use the community's enthusiasm to run special events, such as tournaments, beta testing for new features, or exclusive challenges where players can participate and provide direct feedback on experimental content.
   - Some fan-driven content, like fan art or fan-created movesets, may even inspire official content updates or character designs.

4. **Balancing and Patches**:

- Community feedback regarding balance is especially crucial. Fighting games require continuous adjustments to ensure that no character becomes too dominant or weak. Regular patches are released to tweak character moves, resolve bugs, and improve the overall balance based on player experiences.

9.4 What to Expect in Future Patches

As *Fatal Fury: City of the Wolves* continues to grow, players can expect frequent patches and updates that introduce new content, improve gameplay, and resolve issues. These updates keep the game fresh and engaging, ensuring it stays relevant long after its initial release.

Types of Updates:

1. **Balance Changes**:
   - **Character Tweaks**: Future patches are likely to focus on adjusting the power of specific characters. This can include changes to damage output, movement speed, or move set properties. Developers will adjust these balance issues to maintain fairness and competitiveness within the game.
   - **Matchmaking Improvements**: In online multiplayer modes, future patches may refine matchmaking algorithms to ensure smoother and more balanced online experiences, addressing issues like high latency or unbalanced matchmaking pools.

2. **Bug Fixes**:
   - **Gameplay Fixes**: Developers regularly address issues such as hitbox inconsistencies, frame rate problems, or glitches that can affect gameplay. These patches ensure that the game runs as smoothly as possible, providing a polished experience.
   - **Crash and Stability Fixes**: Players often encounter crashes, especially after new patches or content drops. Expect regular updates that fix these stability issues to avoid frustrating players.

3. **Quality of Life Improvements**:
   - **UI/UX Enhancements**: The interface may receive periodic updates to make navigation easier, improve accessibility, or add new visual features. These updates aim to make the overall player experience more intuitive.
   - **New Features**: Developers may introduce new features based on community requests. These could include new game modes, character customization options, or additional ways to interact with the community (such as integrated replay systems or spectator modes).

4. **Seasonal Events and Updates**:
   - Developers will likely implement seasonal content or limited-time events in future patches. These updates often include special challenges, new costumes, or special bonus items that coincide with holidays or special in-game anniversaries.
   - **Event-Specific Content**: Seasonal updates might introduce unique characters, skins, or special storylines that appear only during certain events, giving players new reasons to log in and engage with the game.

Patch Timetable:

- Patches and content updates will follow a regular timetable, with smaller, bug-fixing updates arriving every few weeks and larger content-focused patches being released every few months. Keep an eye on the game's patch notes or official announcements to stay informed about upcoming changes.

CHAPTER 10: APPENDICES

10.1 Glossary of Terms

Understanding the terminology used in *Fatal Fury: City of the Wolves* can greatly enhance your gameplay experience, whether you're a beginner or an experienced player. This glossary provides definitions for key terms, mechanics, and concepts commonly used in the game.

Key Terminology:

1. **Combo**: A series of consecutive attacks that are performed without the opponent being able to break free. Combos typically involve fast, timed inputs to keep the opponent locked in a sequence of hits.
2. **Super Move**: A powerful, cinematic attack that requires a full special move meter to execute. Super moves are often the most devastating attacks in a fighter's arsenal.
3. **EX Move**: An enhanced version of a character's standard special move, usually involving more damage or unique properties. These moves often require the player to use a portion of the special meter.
4. **Counter Hit**: A hit that connects while the opponent is in the middle of performing their own attack. A counter hit usually deals extra damage or may allow for a combo to continue.
5. **Blocking**: A defensive action where the player holds the controller in a way that their character absorbs the opponent's attack without taking full damage. Blocked attacks may still drain a small amount of health or leave the defender open for a counterattack.

6. **Special Meter**: A bar at the bottom of the screen that fills as the player executes actions. It is used to perform EX and Super Moves. Managing this resource is key to executing powerful attacks.
7. **Stagger**: When a character is hit by a move that temporarily disrupts their movement, leaving them open to follow-up attacks. Staggering can create windows of vulnerability.
8. **Throw**: A special attack that grabs the opponent and throws them across the screen, typically dealing a significant amount of damage and breaking through blocking.
9. **Air Juggle**: A technique that involves keeping the opponent airborne with a series of hits or combos. Air juggles allow for extended combo chains that increase damage output.
10. **Meter Burn**: The use of the special meter during a combo or attack to extend its duration or deal more damage. It is a strategic way of maximizing attack effectiveness.

10.2 Character Move Lists

Each character in *Fatal Fury: City of the Wolves* has a unique set of moves, including normal attacks, special moves, and super moves. Below is a breakdown of typical character move lists, though each fighter will have their own unique set.

Standard Moves:

1. **Light Punch**: A quick jab with low damage but fast recovery, useful for starting combos.
2. **Heavy Punch**: A slower but stronger punch, often used for finishing combos or spacing out opponents.

3. **Light Kick**: A quick, low-risk kick that can be used for poking at an opponent.
4. **Heavy Kick**: A stronger kick, often used in combination with other moves for knockdowns or juggles.

Special Moves:

1. **Fireball (Quarter Circle Forward + Punch)**: A projectile move that travels across the screen, useful for zoning or attacking at mid-range.
2. **Dragon Punch (Forward, Down, Down-Forward + Punch)**: A fast, upward move that hits opponents attempting to jump in. It can be used to interrupt attacks.
3. **Tornado Kick (Quarter Circle Back + Kick)**: A spinning move that hits multiple times. It can be used to close the gap between you and your opponent.
4. **Slide (Down, Down-Forward + Kick)**: A low-moving attack that can slide across the ground, tripping up an opponent or reaching them during their recovery.

Super Moves:

1. **Mega Punch (Double Quarter Circle Forward + Punch)**: A devastating, cinematic attack that deals massive damage when it connects, often with a wide hitbox.
2. **Burning Kick (Quarter Circle Back + Kick, followed by Punch)**: A fast-moving super that uses quick kicks and finishes with a powerful final strike.

EX Moves:

1. **EX Fireball (Quarter Circle Forward + Punch + EX Button)**: A more powerful version of the standard fireball, usually

faster or with additional effects, such as larger hitboxes or multiple hits.

2. **EX Dragon Punch (Forward, Down, Down-Forward + Punch + EX Button)**: A stronger, faster Dragon Punch that may also have invincibility frames.

10.3 Stage and Arena Maps

The arenas in *Fatal Fury: City of the Wolves* are more than just backgrounds—they are integral parts of the gameplay, with unique elements and hazards that can impact matches. Here's an overview of some of the key stages and maps you'll encounter in the game.

Classic Stages:

1. **South Town Streets**:
   - **Description**: The gritty, urban environment of South Town where many of the game's early battles take place. Features dark alleys, neon lights, and a concrete jungle backdrop.
   - **Hazards**: The narrow layout of the street makes it difficult to maneuver, and there are certain spots where obstacles may block attacks or affect player movement.
2. **The Dojo**:
   - **Description**: A traditional dojo with wooden floors and paper walls. This serene setting contrasts with the violence of the battle.
   - **Hazards**: No major hazards, but the narrowness of the stage means players must be more strategic with their movement, especially in longer combo chains.

3. **The Rooftop**:
   - o **Description**: A dramatic rooftop battle set against the skyline of South Town, with a night sky full of stars.
   - o **Hazards**: Occasionally, the wind can affect projectile trajectories, adding a layer of unpredictability.
4. **Underground Fight Club**:
   - o **Description**: A dark, gritty underground setting with a circular arena surrounded by spectators.
   - o **Hazards**: The limited space can make it difficult to avoid heavy attacks, especially when multiple enemies or obstacles come into play.
5. **Tournament Arena**:
   - o **Description**: A professional setting where major tournaments are held, featuring grand stands and high-energy crowds.
   - o **Hazards**: No major hazards, but the pressure of performing in front of a crowd can psychologically affect the player's pacing during battle.

Dynamic Stages:

- **Day/Night Cycle**: Some stages change their appearance and conditions based on whether the battle takes place during the day or night.
- **Interactive Elements**: Certain stages feature interactive elements like collapsing buildings, destructible walls, or obstacles that can influence gameplay.

10.4 Resources and Further Reading

For players who want to dive deeper into *Fatal Fury: City of the Wolves*, there are many resources available to improve your gameplay, learn about the game's mechanics, and stay up-to-date with the latest updates.

Official Sources:

1. **Official Website**: The best place to find official news, patch notes, character guides, and upcoming DLC announcements.
2. **Game Manual**: A comprehensive guide provided with the game that covers controls, mechanics, and other essential features of the game.
3. **Developer Livestreams and Q&A**: Tune in to official streams where developers discuss updates, patch notes, character strategies, and take questions from the community.

Community Resources:

1. **Game Forums**: Sites like Reddit, GameFAQs, and Discord offer spaces where players can discuss strategies, ask questions, and share insights about the game.
2. **YouTube Tutorials**: Plenty of skilled players post tutorials on character moves, combos, and advanced strategies. Watching these can be very useful for improving your gameplay.
3. **Twitch Streams**: Watch high-level players compete in real-time to learn new strategies, moves, and combinations. Streams often feature commentary and tips that can be applied to your own gameplay.

Fan-Made Resources:

1. **Strategy Guides**: Several fan-made guides and eBooks are available online that provide in-depth looks at character moves, advanced tactics, and game mechanics.
2. **Character-Specific Blogs and Wikis**: Many characters have their own dedicated fan sites or wikis that focus on mastering that particular fighter, providing valuable move lists, combo guides, and strategies.

Related Games:

1. **King of Fighters Series**: Since *Fatal Fury* is part of the *King of Fighters* franchise, players can benefit from exploring the crossover content and characters in the *King of Fighters* games.
2. **Samurai Shodown**: A related SNK fighting game that shares similar mechanics and can provide additional insight into SNK's fighting style and character design.